OCCASIONAL CONTRIBUTIONS FROM THE MUSEUM OF ANTHROPOLOGY OF THE UNIVERSITY OF MICHIGAN
No. 11

OLD BIRCH ISLAND CEMETERY

AND THE EARLY HISTORIC TRADE ROUTE

GEORGIAN BAY, ONTARIO

BY
EMERSON F. GREENMAN

ANN ARBOR
UNIVERSITY OF MICHIGAN PRESS
1951

ISBN (print): 978-1-949098-53-2
ISBN (ebook): 978-1-951538-52-1

Browse all of our books at
sites.lsa.umich.edu/archaeology-books.

Order our books from the University of Michigan
Press at www.press.umich.edu.

For permissions, questions, or manuscript queries,
contact Museum publications by email at umma-pubs@umich.edu or visit the Museum website at
lsa.umich.edu/ummaa.

FOREWORD

In 1938 Old Birch Island was in archaeologically unknown territory. The co-operation of several individuals expedited the work of exploration and contributed to the convenience of the members of the field party. Mr. W. J. Wintemberg, now deceased, and Dr. Diamond Jenness, of the National Museum of Canada, gave information about the Manitoulin region and furnished names of residents who could supply information. Mr. Grant Turner of Little Current contributed valuable leads to the locations of sites and was helpful in many other ways.

For consultation and advice on the interpretation of the cultural affiliations of Old Birch Island Cemetery, I am indebted to Dr. William A. Ritchie, of the New York State Museum, Dr. Richard MacNeish, of the National Museum of Canada, and Dr. James B. Griffin, of the University of Michigan. Mr. Robert Benton, a student in 1938, was field assistant. Mr. John Walker, now deceased, and Mr. and Mrs. Gus McGregor, of Birch Island Reserve, contributed information on the history of the Indians of the Manitoulin District and on the locations of archaeological sites.

A grant from the Board of Governors of the Horace H. Rackham School of Graduate Studies made possible the excavation of Old Birch Island Cemetery and also provided for the publication of the results.

Emerson F. Greenman

CONTENTS

ILLUSTRATIONS

PLATES

(Plates I–XXVI follow page 69.)

FIGURES IN THE TEXT

FIGURE

MAPS

MAP

INTRODUCTION

FROM the beginning of systematic investigation of archaeological remains in the Great Lakes region there has been an interest in sites occupied by the Indians while they were in the early stages of contact with Europeans. This interest is based upon the opportunity for dating native Indian materials which occur in graves and pits in direct association with objects of European origin. It is sometimes also possible to assign the native materials to a given Indian group when historic record indicates the presence of the group on the site at which the association occurs.

With these and other considerations in mind an archaeological survey of the Manitoulin District of Ontario was begun in 1938. Very little was known about the archaeology of the region, and there were no publications of the excavations, almost all of which had been casually and unsystematically carried out. The Manitoulin District was chosen partly because it lay along the early historic trade route between Sault Ste Marie and Montreal, used by the Indians and the French between 1608 and 1760.[1]

Much has been written about this ancient canoe route from the early French posts in eastern Canada to Sault Ste Marie and St. Ignace. Publications of a historical nature contain little, however, about conditions along any part of the route, and the remarks of the Jesuits and traders who actually made the trip are confined chiefly to that part of the route occupied by the Ottawa and French rivers. The first question that arose at the beginning of the work in the Manitoulin District was whether the route lay along the north or the south shore of Manitoulin Island, or along the shore of the mainland to the north. On theoretical grounds, taking the limitations of canoe travel into consideration, after a few weeks' experience with the south shore of the island it seemed that it must have had little

[1] *Jesuit Relations*, 50: 249–67; Anonymous, 1855, p. 622; Colden, p. 667; Clare, and others, 1768, p. 26; Cadillac, p. 588.

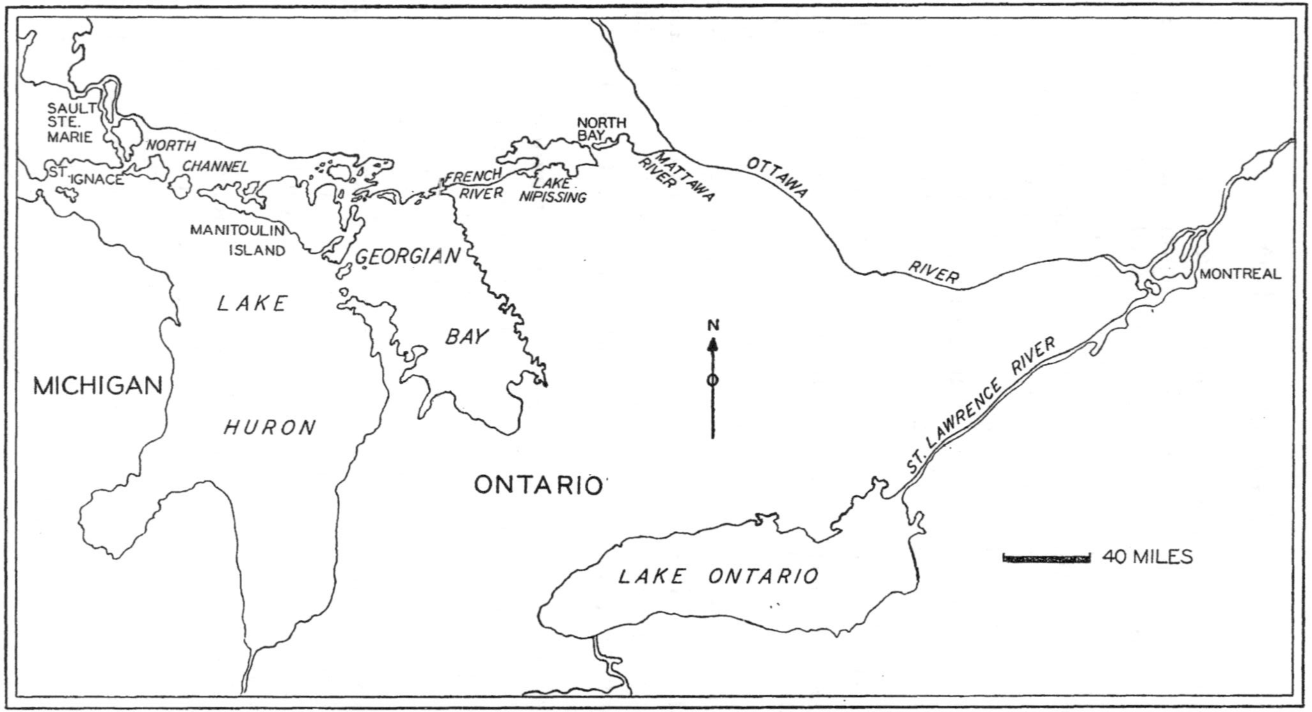

Map 1. Early historic trade route, Sault Ste Marie to Montreal.

if any of the traffic from the mouth of French River either to the Straits of Mackinac or to Sault Ste Marie. The shore is easily accessible, and the bays are deep and protected, but the uninterrupted expanse of Lake Huron to the south makes for rougher shore waters than even the large canoes of the period could have navigated with convenience. The archaeology of the south shore bears out this conclusion. While sandy beaches are numerous, only one had been the scene of aboriginal activities, a pre-Columbian site of the Iroquois Aspect at Providence Bay.[2] All evidences of east-west travel in early historic times, including the 2 sites described herein, are north of Manitoulin Island (Map 1).

The full extent of this water highway was from Montreal up the Ottawa River to Lake Nipissing by way of Mattawa River, from Lake Nipissing to Georgian Bay by way of French River, thence to Killarney and on west into the North Channel, presumably along the north shore to Potagannissing Bay, either entering St. Mary's River or turning south through Detour Passage, depending on whether the destination was Sault Ste Marie or St. Ignace. The north shore of the North Channel was probably followed because there are more islands and fewer wide bays to cross than would be encountered on the north shore of Manitoulin Island.

The part of this trade route for which detailed knowledge was obtained in the years from 1938 to 1950 is a section some 50 miles long between Flat Point on the north shore of North Channel, directly north of Little Current, and Pickerel River, which is the easternmost of the several entrances to French River. Aside from the St. Mary's River approach to Sault Ste Marie, this is the most protected section of the entire route in Georgian Bay. Except for 6 miles of open water it is a devious and rather complex passage through long channels and across bays and between islands of varying size (Map 2).

Today, the east end of the North Channel has 2 openings into Georgian Bay proper, one at Little Current, the other through Cloche Channel and eastward past the northernmost

[2] Greenman, report in preparation.

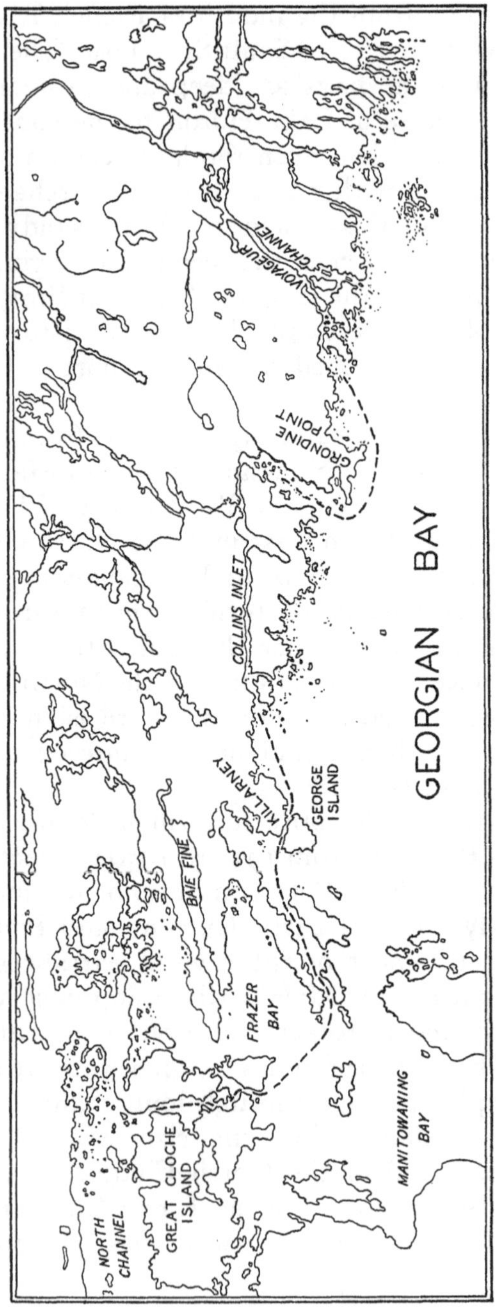

MAP 2. Fifty miles of the early historic trade route, Little Current to French River.

point of Little Cloche Island, though a railroad bridge at Swift Current has so narrowed Cloche Channel at that point as to make it available only to launches and small boats (Pl. II, Fig. 1). At the present time Little Cloche Island is separated from Great Cloche Island by a stony depression about 200 feet wide, which at its center sometimes has water only a few inches deep, but which was deep enough for canoe passage at the time it was first seen in connection with this survey. The marine chart[3] shows Cloche Channel as open to navigation in 1886, and 2 centuries ago water probably filled the entire depression. The channel is only about a mile from the channel at the north end of Little Cloche Island, and no doubt both were used during the heyday of the old trade route. But the presence of early historic remains along the southern outlet, recorded herein as site LC 1,[4] points to it as the one most commonly used. This would be expected, for it is in more direct line to French River. Boats headed for the mouth of this river, upon emerging from the channel, had 4 miles of open water to cross before reaching the west end of Lansdowne Channel and its 10 miles of protected water to Killarney. This is the route now taken by all smaller craft between Killarney and Little Current. The lake steamers take the outside route, to the south of Badgeley Island.

From the west the route continued through Killarney Channel, which is about 2 miles long. Its east end opens into Georgian Bay proper, and one of the most difficult stretches of water of the entire route in stormy weather would have been the 3 miles from this point to the entrance to Collins Inlet, but once that river-like channel (Pl. V, Fig. 2) was reached, the 18 miles to the mouth of Beaverstone Bay would offer no difficulties. The next hazard was the re-entry into Georgian Bay and the rounding of Grondine Point, but Voyageur Channel (Pl. VI), the westernmost entrance to French River, lay only 3 miles beyond; turning quickly to the left, or north, after clearing Grondine Point, protection would be found in shallow waters,

[3] Old Admiralty Chart, No. 1213.

[4] Greenman and Stanley, 1940.

full of shoals but sheltered from the north by the shore and from the east and south by small islands.

Grondine Point, boldly exposed to the 100 miles of open water of Georgian Bay (Pl. V, Fig. 1), was rounded with difficulty in stormy weather. Alexander Henry[5] mentioned this place, which he passed on August 31, 1761, on the way to Michilimackinac: "We passed Pointe de Grondines, so called, from the perpetual noise of the water among the rocks. Many of these rocks are sunken, and not without danger when the wind, as at this time it was, is from the south." The description is completely accurate and indicates that he was probably within 300 feet of the shore. Passage is safer in rough weather on the outside of Grondine Rock, which is about a mile off Grondine Point, and modern traffic goes that way. On his return trip in 1764 the wind forced Henry to put his canoe ashore at Grondine Point at noon on June 15, and he spent the night there.[6] On this occasion he described it as "Pointe aux Grondines." The feature is known locally in the Manitoulin District as "Grumbling Point." Henry made no reference to the size of the canoes he used on the return trip, but those for the trip west in 1761 he described as five and one-half fathoms long, four and a half feet in greatest width, and of birch bark a quarter of an inch thick.[7] There were 8 Indian paddlers to each canoe, and, with the freight, Henry estimated the total weight as about 4 tons.[8] On the return trip in 1764, when he was forced ashore at Grondine Point, he evidently had 2 canoes.[9] In the trip west in 1761 he apparently did not go by way of Collins Inlet, since he stated that after passing Grondine Point, "we coasted along many small islands, or rather rocks, of more or less extent, either wholly bare, or very scantily covered with scrub pine trees. All the land to the northward is of the same description, as high as Cha'ba'bou'an'ing, where verdure reappears."[10] The place referred to is Killarney. The Ojibway term is in use

[5] Henry, 1809, p. 33. [6] *Ibid.*, p. 175.

[7] *Ibid*, pp. 13–14. Paddles rather than oars were used, and sails were sometimes employed.

[8] *Ibid.*, p. 15. [9] *Ibid.*, p. 173. [10] *Ibid.*, p. 33.

today and is translated as "channel." The route from Grondine Point to Killarney is known today as the "Inside Passage" and is taken by those familiar with the shoals. There is no mention of the use of the Collins Inlet route in early historic times, but the Indians must have known of it.

About a mile north of Grondine Point on the Beaverstone Bay side, a small arm of that bay extends eastward, penetrating the Grondine Peninsula for a distance of about 2 miles. Although it is not on any map, a wide slough extends from the east side of the Grondine Peninsula to within probably less than a quarter of a mile of the end of the small arm of Beaverstone Bay. It is some 500 feet wide, and the ground which prevents it from going clear through to the west side of the peninsula is at its highest point little more than 5 feet above the water level. The map shows a very short stream at the eastern end of the slough, but the level of the slough appears to be the same as that of Georgian Bay. On the north side of the mouth, on a strip of sand adjoining a ridge of rock, there is a small pre-Columbian site, French River site No. 1,[11] from which a stone celt and a few very small fragments of pottery, probably Woodland in type, were collected in 1947. The site in 1947 was 4.7 feet above the level of Georgian Bay and should, by the post-Nipissing chronology,[12] have been under water 300 years ago. Such a state would not be incompatible with the lack of European goods. Some of these may be found after more intensive excavation. In any event, not long before the beginning of the historic period there was an inlet through the base of the Grondine Peninsula, which would have accommodated coastwise travel by canoe. The site at its eastern end may owe its origin to this geographical feature (Map 3).[13]

There are 6 entrances to French River from Georgian Bay. They are known, from west to east, as Voyageur Channel, Black Bay, Bad River Channel, French River (main outlet), French

[11] Greenman, report in preparation.

[12] Greenman and Stanley, 1940, pp. 198–99.

[13] It is rather suggestive that the area where the slough enters Georgian Bay is a small shallow cove recorded as "Indian Bight" on the Old Admiralty Chart, No. 1213.

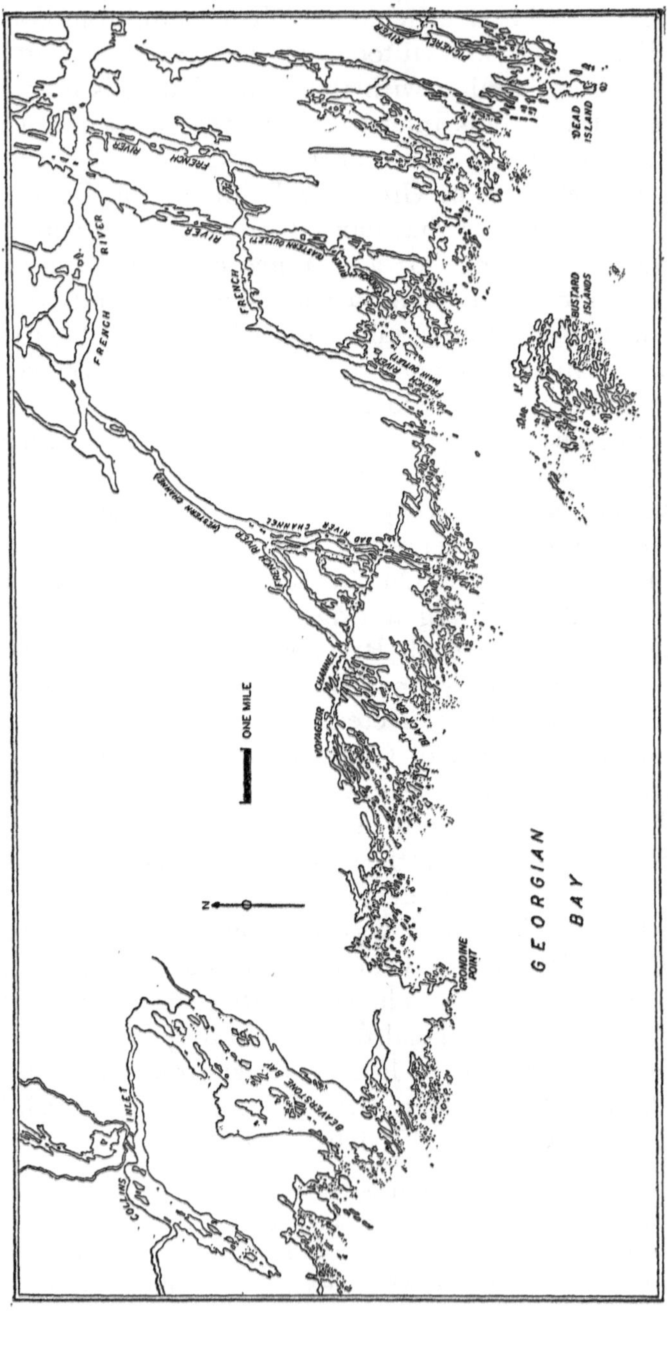

Map 3. The outlets of French River.

River (eastern outlet), and Pickerel River. These entrances are separated by intervals of 2 to 3 miles and extend along some 12 miles of the coast, from a point east of Grondine Peninsula to the mouth of Pickerel River. The coast line here, as all the way from Killarney, is broken up by innumerable small islands, rocks, and reefs, and the entrances to French River are difficult to find, with the exception of the main entrance, which is a mile wide (Pl. VII, Fig. 2; Pl. III, Fig. 1). This channel is navigable for craft of any size for about 4 miles, to a point where there is a fall of some 9 feet. The other channels can be entered only in small boats, and anyone unfamiliar with the route would experience considerable difficulty in getting through to the point where French River turns eastward. The name now borne by the westernmost of these entrances, Voyageur Channel, suggests its use in early historic times by the French and Indians. Voyageur Channel, Black Bay, and Bad River Channel all converge to form a stretch of water 3 miles long and nearly half a mile wide. Information has been received of archaeological features along its shores, but no investigation has yet been made.

Place names and archaeological sites support the foregoing interpretation of the course of the old trade route from the east end of the North Channel to French River. The only early historic sites found in the Manitoulin District are on Cloche Island and on Old Birch Island at the entrance to McGregor Bay (Map 4). French place names favor the northern route. There is only one such name (Frechette Bay) on the south shore of Manitoulin Island, directly south of Bayfield Sound. All major features of the landscape at the east end of the North Channel are named *cloche* ("bell"): La Cloche Mountains, Great and Little Cloche islands, Cloche Peninsula, and Cloche Channel. Apparently, the first so named was Cloche Island; the legend connected with this is recorded by Henry.[14] Baie Fine is another French place name applied to the long river-like bay which parallels McGregor Point on the south. Baie de Foie is not named on the maps of the region, but is used locally for a small

[14] Henry, 1809, p. 33.

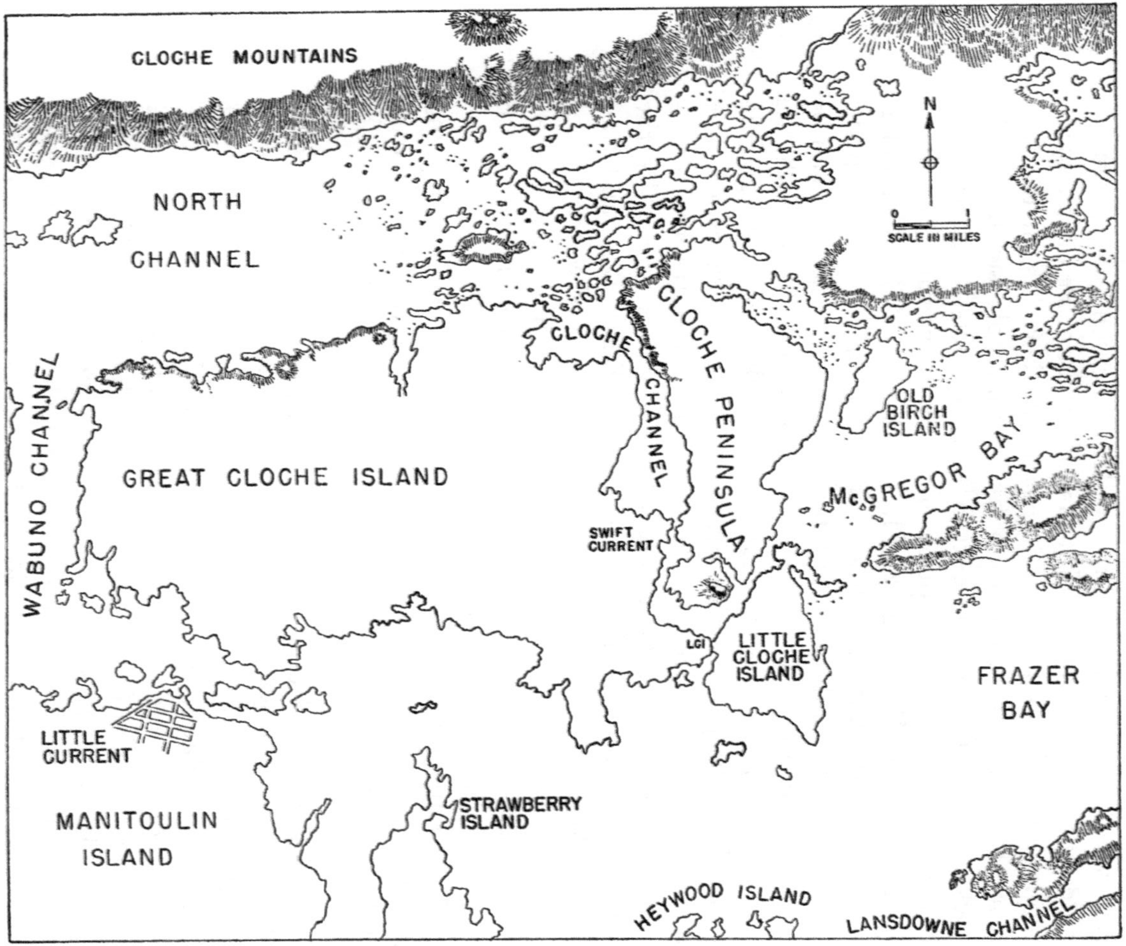

Map. 4. North Channel, McGregor Bay and Frazer Bay, and Old Birch Island. Dreamer's Rock is a quartzite knob at the southern tip of Cloche Peninsula.

indentation of the coast just east of Killarney, and Lamorandière Bay, the official designation of the narrow part at the end of Killarney Bay, derives its name from the family that first settled at Killarney.

The locations of early trading posts also have a bearing on the line of travel. A post of the Northwest Company was situated at the northwest corner of Great Cloche Island, at what is now known as Northwest Point, and the remains of a Hudson Bay trading post are still to be seen directly north of there on the north shore. Other ruins, said to be of a trading post, are on what is locally known as "Jumbo Bay" at the north end of Cloche Channel. According to a tradition in the Manitoulin area the earlier route was through Cloche Channel and the later one was through Wabuno Channel at the west end of Great Cloche Island, and past Little Current. This route may have become feasible at the introduction of sturdier boats, for there is a long stretch of open water from Little Current to Center Island at the entrance to Lansdowne Channel.[15] Place names in Ojibway provide little or no information on the early route, although it is of interest that Iroquois Island is at the head of McGregor Bay.

[15] See Maps 2 and 4. The early historic trade route is indicated as entering Lansdowne Channel at the southern end of Frazer Bay, and continuing on to Killarney Channel.

SITES IN THE VICINITY OF OLD BIRCH ISLAND

In the summer of 1938 two early historic sites were located. The first, on Great Cloche Island, was evidently the cemetery of the village mentioned by Henry[16] as one of his stopping places. Excavation of this cemetery had been carried on previously for many years, and nothing was left of the original graves, which were on a ridge of sand extending about 500 feet east and west, 3 feet high, and 40 feet wide (Pl. X, Fig. 1). This ridge is a raised beach, deposited on the limestone surface at a time when the waters of Lake Huron were 28 feet higher than they are today, and it was at the unexcavated eastern end that the first of the sites connected with post-Nipissing beaches was found.[17] European materials from this site are in the collections of Mr. Grant Turner and Mrs. M. Trotter, of Little Current. A few glass beads and brass bangles were found on the surface by the Museum of Anthropology field party and are described in this report.

In August, during excavation of the Old Birch Island site, information was received from Mr. John Walker of Birch Island Reserve that refuse material and signs of historic occupation were to be seen at the southern end of the small channel which separates Great Cloche Island and Little Cloche Island, about one quarter of a mile south of the ridge, on Great Cloche Island. Walker served as guide to this spot (Pl. IV, Fig. 2), and a number of beads and a brass bangle were collected in the 3 to 6 inches of moss on the rock surface. This area was evidently the camping site, and the cemetery was on the ridge of sand to the north, as indicated by the presence of burials of the historic period. Lack of sufficient soil for the growing of crops suggests that this site was no more than a temporary stopping place along a route of travel or that its inhabitants lived altogether by hunting and fishing. The finding of small fragments of pottery and of flakes of quartzite and flint a quarter of a mile west of the cemetery on a sand ridge at the same elevation as that

[16] Henry, 1809, pp. 33–34, 175.

[17] Greenman and Stanley, 1940.

of the cemetery indicates occupation in precontact times, perhaps more or less continuously since the time of the camp site beneath the rubble at the east end of the ridge on which the cemetery is situated.

In August, 1761, when Alexander Henry visited Great Cloche Island, he reported the presence of a large village of Indians,[18] which was probably the one represented by the site under discussion. The Ojibway name for this site was given as ʌ sin'dewe[19] and translated as "Bell Rock" by John Walker and other informants. This term refers to the reputed capacity of certain rocks on this island to give a ringing sound when struck, a story which has persisted to the present, with the result that several of the quartzite boulders on the surface of the limestone (Pl. X, Fig. 2) have been struck so often with axes or smaller rocks that they are in fragments. One rock within 400 feet of the area where the glass beads and bangles were found stands on end to a height of about 5 feet (Pl. II, Fig. 2). On its top are 5 circular cuplike depressions, .3 to .4 foot in diameter and from .2 to .3 foot deep. They are in a straight line nearly east and west, and .2 to .4 foot from the edge of one to the edge of the next. A dozen or more similar holes of somewhat smaller dimensions are elsewhere on the top and sides of this rock. The origin of these depressions is uncertain. They are fresh in appearance and, unlike the natural surface of the rock, are not covered with lichen growths. If they date from the period of occupation of this site nearly 200 years ago, the appearance of having recently been pecked out would hardly be expected.

[18] Henry, 1809, p. 33.

[19] For phonetic symbols used, see Bloomfield, 1933, pp. 547–49.

OLD BIRCH ISLAND CEMETERY

Old Birch Island is a designation probably given by Ojibway Indians who lived at the south end of the island three-quarters of a century or more ago.[20] Later, this group of Indians moved to the mainland directly west (Pl. I, Fig. 1), where the foundations of log houses are still to be seen. This village also was abandoned, and the descendants of the occupants now live at the head of the western arm of McGregor Bay, where a ridge of limestone about 100 feet high separates McGregor Bay from the North Channel. This is the Birch Island Reserve.

Old Birch Island is a limestone ridge nearly 2 miles long and about one-half mile wide, rising at its center to a height of some 200 feet. Its lower slopes are densely wooded with maple, oak, balm of Gilead, and birch, with spruce and cedar in the swampy areas. The top of the island is covered with white pine and Norway pine. Old Birch Island is crown land and has no permanent inhabitants.

At the south and north ends sand to a depth of 3 feet or more along the shore, extending inland some 300 feet, forms level terraces several acres in extent. The southern terrace is reportedly the site of the village of Indians before their departure to the mainland, but an examination of the surface and a few test pits failed to reveal any sign of early historic or pre-Columbian occupancy.

At the north end of the island the water-washed light brown sand extends from the northernmost tip southward about 700 feet, reaching an elevation of 15 feet above lake level at its southern termination, where it gives way to coarser dark red sand mixed with rounded pebbles. On the terrace of light brown sand where its surface is 8 to 12 feet above the lake level, numerous pits had been dug (Fig. 3). Their existence has long been known to the residents of Birch Island Reserve. The pits are 2 to 4 feet deep and 4 to 10 feet in diameter. A brief examination of the sides and bottoms revealed no refuse material of any sort to give a clue to their purpose. They are, perhaps,

[20] Old Birch Island is known locally as "Wardrop Island."

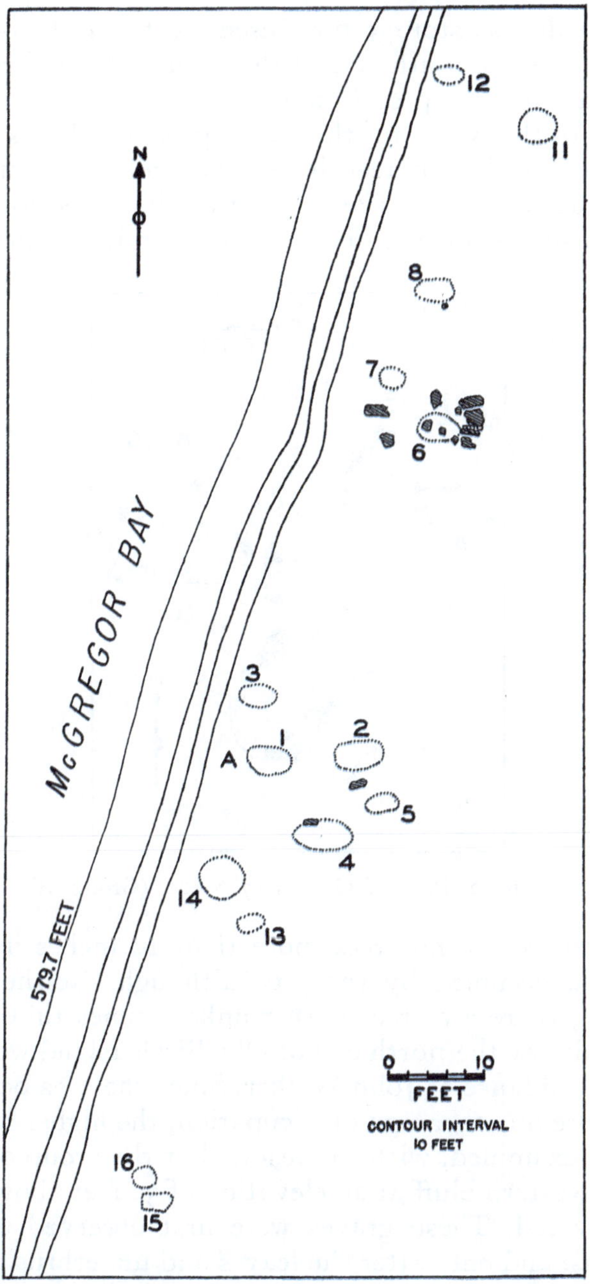

FIG. 1. Plan of Graves 1 to 16 (Group A). Shading indicates boulders. Dotted line represents outline of the depression over the grave.

to be regarded as storage pits, used by the Indians who formerly lived at the south end of the island. One informant suggested that this group of Indians may have cut timber at the north end of the island for the steam-propelled boats that plied these waters in the nineteenth century, and then planted crops on the land thus cleared and dug the pits for storage of produce from such plantings. This explanation is supported by the

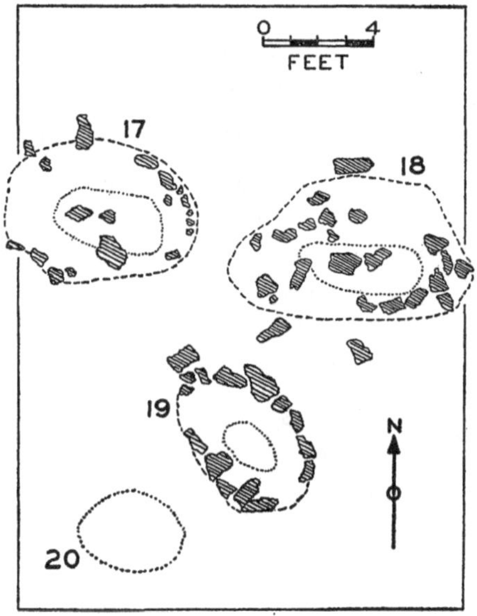

FIG. 2. Plan of Graves 17 to 20 (Group B).

fact that there are no trees more than 10 inches in diameter in the area occupied by the pits, although elsewhere, at the same level, there are trees with trunks 4 times that diameter.

These pits at the north end of Old Birch Island were visited under the guidance of John Walker. Since the area occupied by the pits bore no other sign of occupation, the higher land to the south was examined, with the result that the group of 4 graves along the western bluff at an elevation of 32 feet above the lake was discovered. These graves were first observed as shallow depressions, and only after the leaves and underbrush had been cleared away did it become apparent that the limestone boulders scattered about had been placed there intentionally. Subsequently, 12 other depressions were found along the edge of the bluff (Fig. 1). After these depressions had been excavated, 4 additional graves (17–20) were disclosed 225 feet to the east, at an elevation of 20 feet above the level of the lake (Fig. 2).

These 2 groups of graves—the 16 comprising Group A, along the edge of the bluff, and the 4 comprising Group B, at the

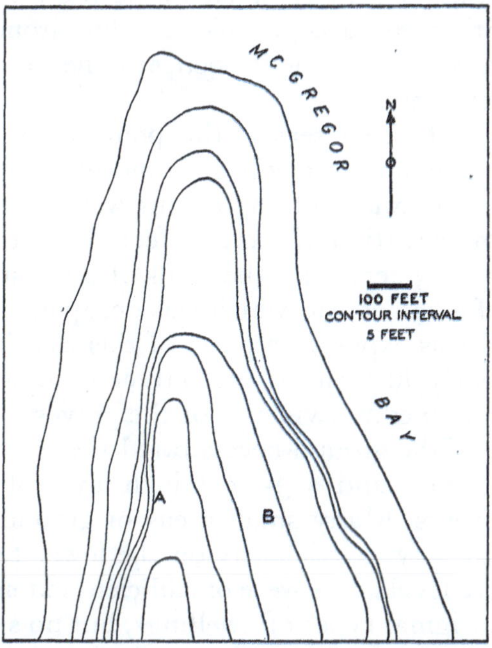

FIG. 3. The 2 sets of graves at Old Birch Island. Group A is on higher ground than Group B.

lower level to the east (Fig. 3)—were probably not contemporaneous. One object, a silver gorget with the touchmark "R C" (Pl. XXII, Fig. 1B) dates the grave in which it was found as after 1770, and by implication the other 3 graves (1 of which was empty) may have been of the same period. It is possible that the graves along the bluff are earlier. Of the total of 20 graves, or artificial depressions, 7 of the first group and 1 in the second group contained no remains. Although there were many natural depressions in the vicinity of both groups which approximated the graves in size and shape, the artificial origin of these 7 was confirmed by the presence in each instance of a slightly elevated ring of excavated materials. Two of these depressions in the earlier group of graves along the bluff, Graves 9 and 10, were 100 feet south of Grave 5, and are not shown in Figure 1. No boulders were around any of these empty graves, nor were any in such a position as to indicate a connection with them, except a block of limestone about 1 foot square, which was a few inches beneath the bottom of Grave 20 of the lower group.

The presence of a cemetery at this point on Old Birch Island suggested the remains of a village somewhere in the vicinity. The nearest level ground of any extent was about 1000 feet to the south at an elevation of some 50 feet above the lake, where a clearing of 2 to 3 acres and the ruins of 2 log structures were the remains of a homestead which was occupied about the year 1915. The soil was exposed in parts of this clearing, but no indications of early historic or precontact occupation were observed. In the immediate vicinity of the graves an examination of the surface of the ground necessitated the removal of underbrush, dead leaves, and a 3- to 6-inch layer of closely intertwined small roots. Many small areas of ground surface were sampled in this way, particularly on the lower terraces east of the bluff, where level areas were of sufficient extent to allow the erection of aboriginal types of dwellings, but no signs of domestic activities were seen. The only object found on the surface, well away from any grave, was a stone bar (Pl. XXII, Fig. 2F). It came from a point 3 feet east of the east end of Grave 3. There was nothing to suggest that the group of Indians whose members were buried in this cemetery had lived on Old Birch Island.

Many references have been made to the practice, among the Indian tribes of Canada and the United States in early and middle historic times, of erecting small enclosures of wood over graves. Graves are still to be seen at Bay Mills, Chippewa County, Michigan, and elsewhere, in which the collapsed remains of structures of sawn timbers lie in and around the edges of depressions similar in size and shape to the depression over each of the burials on Old Birch Island. In excavating the burials, however, the presence of a ring of earth around each depression at the surface of the ground (Fig. 4) indicated that the depressions were not caused by disintegration of perishable objects in the grave, but that they were holes that had not been

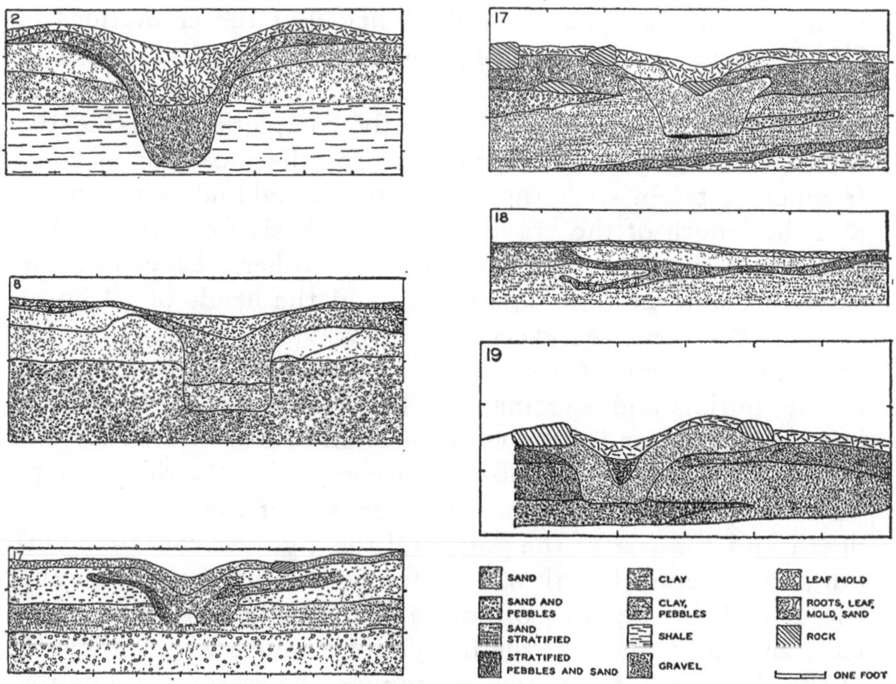

FIG. 4. Cross sections of Graves 2, 8, 17, 18, and 19

filled. At Old Birch Island there was no evidence of small burial houses above the ground over the grave. Apparently, the burials lay in rectangular boxlike chambers made of wooden slabs, with a covering of the same material at or below the ground level (see Graves 1, 8, 17). In most instances the topmost part of the skull was the uppermost point of the burial. As much as .7 foot of earth covered the skulls, but the average thickness of the earth was about .3 foot. Either the burials were intentionally covered with .1 to .7 foot of earth, or the earth dropped on the burial with the collapse of a covering. That the tops of the skulls of 3 burials (Graves 4, 5, 15) were not covered suggests that at the time of completion of the burials the graves were left unfilled.

Old Birch Island Cemetery (including both groups of graves) contained the remains of 16 individuals in 12 graves. This number is based upon the probability that the cremations in Graves 3 and 15 comprised the remains of other individuals than those represented in the same graves by uncremated bones. All but 3 skeletons were sufficiently complete to enable the establishment of the position at once; the locations of skull fragments, taken with the age of the individual represented, and the length of the grave provided a basis for a reasonably accurate estimate of the positions of 2 others. Eleven of the skeletons were more or less flexed, and the heads of all but 1 were to the west; the exception, in Grave 13, had the head a little to the north of east. One grave (Grave 15) contained 3 bundle burials and a cremation. The long bones of the bundle burials lay east and west, with the skull of one to the east and of the other to the west. No skull accompanied the third group. There was a correspondence between age of the individual at death and the size of the grave. Of the 3 graves containing infants, the average length was 2.9 feet; of the 6 graves containing the articulated remains of adults, the average length was 3.7 feet, and the longest of the 6 was more than twice the length of the shortest of the graves containing the remains of infants.

Depths of the graves varied from 1 foot to 2.7 feet. In the higher part of the site, along the ridge (Fig. 3 A), the soil profile had 3 divisions: at the surface about .6 foot of medium gray sand; this rested on .7 to 1 foot of red gravel containing clay of the same color; beneath this was a deposit of undetermined thickness of soft shale similar in color and constituents to the stratum immediately above. Some of the graves extended into this underlying stratum of shale (Graves 1–4, 8, 13) and the top of this stratum formed the bottom of others (Graves 5, 6, 15; Graves 7, 9–12, 14, 16, which contained no burials).

Attempts were made during excavation to establish a relative chronology of the graves by examining the overlapping of the rings of earth around each open grave, but the graves were too far apart to allow such a condition.

BURIALS

Grave 1 (Pl. XVI, Fig. 1). Depth, 1.9 feet; length, 3.2 feet; width, 1.3 to 1.8 feet; depth of fill, 1.2 feet.[21] The closely flexed skeleton of a person of 18 to 20 years, sex indeterminate, on right side, head to west, facing southeast, with the left arm flexed, radius and ulna across abdomen, right arm tightly flexed. Back of the skull (.3 foot west) lay a large quartzite boulder. Upper part of skull in fragments, probably due to weight of the earth. This grave extended from .4 to .6 foot into the shale substratum, the top of which was 1.3 to 1.9 feet below the surface of the ground.

Along the north and south sides of this grave were vertical layers of badly decayed wood, representing boards .3 foot thick and as long as the grave. This decayed wood was not noted above the level of the top of the shale. The 2 layers slanted toward the bottom of the grave. The presence of small sections of rotted wood and loose sand at each end suggested that boards had also been placed there. Strips of decayed wood lay over the greater part of the skeleton, extending from the west end to within 1.3 feet of the east end. Part of the brass kettle which lay immediately to the south of the vertebral column was also covered with bark. No bark was over the skull. The top (that is, uppermost portion) of the skull was about .1 foot below the bottom of the unfilled upper hole.

Artifacts.[22] These localized into 4 groups.

Group 1: Glass beads, at the proximal end of the left tibia, concentrated mostly in a position adjoining the anterior surface at the tuberosity in a deposit about .1 foot in diameter.[23]

[21] Depth of fill refers to the depth below the surface of the depression over each grave. Depths are, in all instances, maximum and refer to the nearest natural ground surface. Since the area of the group of graves along the bluff sloped about 4 feet from south to north, a datum plane was not used. Occasionally, the surface of the ground at one side of a grave was .5 foot or more lower than that on the other side. In such instances depths were taken from the mean between the two.

[22] See Figure 5 for positions of artifacts in Graves 1, 3, 5, 6, 13, 15, 17, and 19.

[23] See pp. 53–55 for catalogue numbers of beads for each grave.

A few were also at the anterior part of the distal end of the femur. Of the beads thus noted at the left knee 958 are small white beads (No. 21733)[24] and 2 are blue (No. 21733).

Group 2: Glass beads in the occipital region of the skull, distributed mostly from a point .2 foot vertically below the left parietal boss to the sagittal suture, and from there more sparsely to and beneath the mandible. The beads in this position totaled 387 (Nos. 21722, 21732).

Group 3: A small brass pail, lying in the abdominal area immediately to the south of the vertebral column. Inside this pail lay the pieces of a small wooden dish (Pl. XVII, Fig. 3B, No. 21720), which contained a deposit of vegetable materials.

Group 4: The artifacts were in an area about 1.8 feet square beneath the mandible and adjacent parts of the skull, immediately to the north. Objects of iron: 1 chisel or gouge (Pl. XIX, Fig. 1G, No. 21737); 1 blade of a curved knife (Pl. XIX, Fig. 1F, No. 21738); 1 strike-a-light (Pl. XIX, Fig. 1B, No. 21736), lying beneath a bone harpoon (Pl. XVIII, Fig. 2E, No. 21734); part of an iron knife blade (No. 21735), above south end of harpoon (Pl. XVIII, Fig. 2E). Objects of brass: 1 strip of brass on stone punch (Pl. XXII, Fig. 2C, No. 21723); 1 piece of brass (Pl. XXII, Fig. 2E, No. 21727). Objects of stone: 1 limestone punch (Pl. XXII, Fig. 2D, No. 21723) with a piece of brass (Pl. XXII, Fig. 2E, No. 21727) beneath it; 1 double-pointed slate spindle (Pl. XXII, Fig. 2A, No. 21725; 1 circular sandstone disk, incised (Pl. XXI, C–D, No. 21726); 1 flint for use with a strike-a-light (Pl. XXIII, F, No. 21728). Objects of bone: 1 portion of beaver jaw, unworked (No. 21724) and 4 harpoons of bone or antler (Pl. XVIII, Fig. 2B–E, Nos. 21729, 21730, 21729, 21734, respectively). One flint chip, perhaps not

[24] All catalogue numbers are those of the Museum of Anthropology, University of Michigan.

The use of the term "grave" in connection with the 8 empty holes of this cemetery, the descriptions of which follow, is not based upon their possession of any features indicating that they were dug for burial purposes. All of the burials were beneath open holes of the same character as these 8, but it can only be supposed that the latter had any connection with burial operations.

an intentional deposit in the grave, lay at the bottom (No. 21742).

Grave 2 (Pl. XII, Fig. 1). Length, 4.2 feet; width, 1.2 feet; depth of fill, 1.3 feet. The flexed skeleton of a young adult female, lying on back, head to west, forearms lying across abdomen, legs flexed upward so that knees were 1.0 to 1.3 feet above the bottom of the grave. There were no indications that the grave had been lined with wood or bark, or that there had been a covering of such materials, although the upper part was open. On the north side of the skeleton, extending from the feet to the left elbow, was a heavy deposit of small pin cherry seeds, placed there by burrowing animals.

Artifacts. At a distance of .6 foot to the north of the left innominate bone lay a bone awl (Pl. XVIII, Fig. 2A, No. 21744).

Grave 3 (Pl. XI, Fig. 2; Pl. XII, Fig. 2). Depth, 2.3 feet; length, 3.0 feet; width, 1.8 feet; depth of fill, 1.6 feet. The flexed skeleton of a male 60 years of age or over, on left side, head to west, facing north. The right arm was flexed, hand bones near the mandible, left arm less flexed, forearm across abdomen. The cremated remains of a second individual lay in a pile 1.2 feet long, between the leg bones and the north edge of the grave. Along the north side of the grave from one end to the other was a continuous layer of rotten wood .2 foot thick; traces of a similar layer were on the south side, indicating that the sides of the grave had been lined with boards. Strips of bark were also directly over the skeleton, suggesting either a covering of bark or a collapsed slab originally at the ground surface.

Artifacts. This was one of the 2 graves in which there were artifacts in the upper, unfilled part. About 4 inches above the bottom of the unfilled part of the grave, in tangled roots and leaf mold, lay a brass spoon (Pl. XVIII, Fig. 1A, No. 21746) and a worked piece of flint (Pl. XXIII, D, No. 21747), which was probably used as a strike-a-light. On the sloping south side of the grave, .7 foot below the surface, was a tobacco-pipe bowl in effigy of a human being (Pl. XXI, A–B, No. 21750). This pipe lay on the sand on the side of the grave about the center of the long axis, with the face of the effigy to the south, the base to the west. On the sand of the north slope of the grave lay another piece of worked flint at a depth of .9 foot below the surface (Pl. XXIII, A, No. 21751). At the bottom of the west slope and 1 foot north of the pipe lay a water-worn sandstone pebble whetstone about .3 foot long, the long axis east-west (Pl. XXII, Fig. 2B, No. 21749). Among the intertwined roots and in the leaf mold of this hole there were quantities of pin cherry seeds of the type found in Grave 2. The following artifacts were in the grave proper, in direct association with the skeleton: at the right shoulder the top of a bag of cloth and leather (Pl. XI, Fig. 2, No. 21757); directly in front of the facial bones was a brass pail (No. 21758) beneath which lay a circular piece of bark, part of a bark layer preserved by its proximity to the brass; near the right elbow was an iron axe in vertical position, edge down and at the level of the bones of the arm (Pl. XXI, E); across the abdomen was an iron knife (Pl. XIX, Fig. 2C, No. 21754), traces of the wooden handle of which were still in place. In the brass pail were part of a wooden ladle (Pl. XVII, Fig. 3A, No. 21759), a ladle of turtle shell (Pl. XVIII, Fig. 1B, No. 21760), 3 lumps of organic matter, and a lump of grass or hair which lay in the turtle shell ladle. Beneath the brass pail a fragment of cloth was preserved by contact with the brass.

Grave 4. Depth, 1.8 feet; length, 4.0 feet; width, 1.6 feet; depth of fill, 1.6 feet. A large limestone boulder lay on the north side of the open hole, its top within .8 foot from the surface of the ground. This rock was 1.3 feet long, .4 foot thick and .9 foot wide. It lay on edge, long axis east-west (Fig. 1). Another piece of limestone about half this size on the bottom of the hole was not visible until after removal of the leaf mold and roots. In the grave was the skeleton of a young adult male, lying on the back, arms and legs tightly flexed, head to west, facing north. The legs were so flexed that the heels rested near the pubic arch, with the tibiae lying at an angle toward the sides of the grave from the femora. A strip of bark or decayed wood, 1.6 feet long and .3 foot wide, extended from the east end of the unfilled part of the grave along the south side. The top of the skull and part of the pelvis lay at or slightly above the bottom of the upper unfilled hole.

Artifacts. The only artifact was a short iron tube resembling .1 foot of a gun barrel. This was found half a foot from the west end of the unfilled hole, within .3 foot of the bottom (No. 21763).

GRAVE 5. Depth, 1.7 feet; length, 3.4 feet; width, 1.6 feet; depth of fill, 1.7 feet. The dimensions are those of the unfilled hole, since the bottom of the grave was on the shale, and the remains were covered only by earth at the bottom of the west slope of the hole. Three parts of skull plates of an infant were all that remained of the burial. These were at the west end on the surface of the shale.

Artifacts. Distributed on the northeast side of the skull fragments were 832 glass beads in an area .8 foot in diameter. Some of these were displaced and thrown out by trowel before their presence was noted, but all were recovered. There were 805 small discoidal white beads (Nos. 21770, 21771), 7 of the same shape and size but blue (Nos. 21770, 21771), 1 small discoidal black bead (No. 21770) and 19 tubular blue beads (Pl. XXVI, G, No. 21770). One brass bangle was lying on a skull plate (Pl. XX, Fig. 1C, No. 21765), and 2 others lay .1 foot west of the skull plate, .1 foot apart (No. 21769). With its tip .1 foot north of the skull was a small pointed object of catlinite (Pl. XX, Fig. 1E, No. 21766). Half a foot northeast of the skull plate were 2 brass buttons lying .2 foot apart (Pl. XX, Fig. 1B, No. 21767).

GRAVE 6 (Pl. XIII, Fig. 1). Depth, 1.8 feet; length, 3.4 feet; width, 1.9 feet; depth of fill, 1.0 foot. The fragments of the skull of an infant whose milk teeth had not yet completely erupted at death lay within 1.0 foot of the west end of the grave, .4 foot from the south side, at a depth of 1.6 feet. Apparently, it lay on the right side and faced southeast. No other bones were in this grave. This was the only grave of the group along the bluff in connection with which boulders had been placed in any semblance of a general plan (Fig. 1). Eight blocks of limestone were ranged around the east and north sides, and 2 others were in the unfilled hole. Two more large boulders lay on the surface about 3 feet west of the west end of the grave. The possibility that the original skeleton (or the skull if that was all that was placed in the grave) was covered with bark is suggested by the presence of a round disk of bark under a small brass pail which lay next to the skull. The bark beneath the pail and for a distance of 1.4 feet west had been preserved by chemical action of the brass. The pail at the time of its exposure had the appearance of a vessel made of bark, owing to the fact that an overlying strip of bark (either over the entire grave or over the pail only) had fallen around the pail and assumed its contours. Presumably, the bark was part of the original covering over the unfilled part of the grave. Another strip of bark, 1.0 foot long and .5 foot wide, lay with the long axis southwest-northeast, along the north edge of the grave, partly covering a large pewter disk.

Artifacts. The brass pail (Pl. XVII, Fig. 2A, No. 21774) lay adjoining the skull fragments, to the northeast of them. Inside the pail were a small wooden cup (Pl. XVII, Fig. 2B, No. 21777) and a fragile piece of wood shaped like half the bowl of a spoon, but which may not have been worked artificially in any way (Pl. XVIII, Fig. 1C, No. 21772). There were 2 groups of glass beads in the grave, one along the south side 1.4 feet from the west end, in an area .2 foot in diameter. In this group there was a total of 615: 177 as in Plate XXV, Figure 2D; 2 as in Plate XXV, Figure 2C; and 436 as in Plate XXVI, K. The other group of beads (No. 21776) was in an area .3 foot in diameter 1 foot from the west end of the grave on the northern edge, lying partly beneath a circular lead or pewter gorget or disk (Pl. XXII, Fig. 1A, No. 21773). There were 280 of the type in Plate XXV, Figure 2D; and 8 as in Plate XXVI, K. The pewter disk partly overlaid this deposit of beads.

Grave 7. Depth, 1.5 feet; length, 2.5 feet east-west; width, 2.2 feet north-south; depth of fill, 1.5 feet. This grave contained no burial. No indications were found that it had been excavated below the bottom of the open hole.

Grave 8 (Pl. XIII, Fig. 2). Depth, 2.7 feet; length, 3.3 feet; width, 1.1 feet; depth of fill, .9 foot. The skeleton of a youth of 17 to 20 years closely flexed, on the left side facing north, head to the west. Both arms were flexed, the bones of the hands lying near the mandible. The top of the skull was .8 foot below the top of the shale, into which the grave had been dug to a maximum depth of 1.5 feet. The skull was crushed. Indications that the grave had been lined were the presence of rotted wood along the south side for a distance of 2.3 feet paralleling the right humerus and along the east end. These 2 layers were about .1 foot thick; neither rose above the top of the shale into which the grave penetrated.

Artifacts. Ten barrel-shaped beads made of marine conch shell were in a position anterior to the cervical vertebrae suggesting that at the time of burial they formed a string suspended from the neck (Pl. XX, Fig. 2, No. 21780). On the opposite side of the bones of the neck were 3 glass beads; 1 is spheroidal and light blue (Pl. XX, Fig. 1G, No. 21780) and 2 are 10-sided and of a somewhat darker blue (Pl. XXVI, Q, No. 21780).

Grave 9. Depth, 1.7 feet; length, 2.9 feet; width, 2.5 feet. This hole did not extend beneath the shale. There was no burial. The grave was 100 feet south of Grave 5 (Fig. 1) within a short distance of Grave 10.

Grave 10. Depth, 1.9 feet; length, 3.8 feet north-south; width, 3.3 feet east-west; depth of fill, 1.5 feet; 95 feet south of Grave 5 (Fig. 1). A hole had been dug here 1.2 feet into the shale, which was nearer the surface in this area than in the vicinity of Graves 1 to 6. On the south edge of Grave 10 at the level of the top of the shale, there was a notched projectile point of flint, which has a coating of red ochre on both faces (Pl. XXIII, G, No. 21782).

Grave 11. Depth, .9 foot; diameter, 3.0 feet. There was no burial.

Grave 12. Depth, 1.0 foot; length, 3 feet east-west; width, 2.2 feet north-south. There was no burial.

Grave 13 (Pl. XIV). Depth, 1.8 feet; length, 2.0 feet east-west; width, 1.1 feet; depth of fill 1.1 feet. The fragmentary remains of the skeleton of an infant less than 5 years old lay with skull (crushed) at the east end of the grave. Traces and fragments of the leg bones suggested a flexion. A layer of birch bark extended the entire length of the skeleton on the south side, from the edge of the skeleton to a line .4 foot beyond it. The skull lay on the left side, facing southeast. The mandible was out of articulation .5 foot west of the maxilla. Some post-burial disturbance was suggested by this and by the fact that traces of an articulated femur and tibia, flexed, lay to the north of the central axis of the skeleton, whereas the skull faced southeast. It is not impossible that this was a secondary burial, though the presence of ribs would suggest otherwise. This grave did not extend into the shale.

Artifacts. Immediately south of the maxilla in an area .3 foot long and .15 foot wide, were 14 blue glass beads, each bearing a painted design; on one side is a crescent moon with face and 2 stars, on the other side 3 stars, one of which has a serpentine streamer (Pl. XXIV, Figs. 1, 2; Pl. XXVI, N, O). Three of these beads lay beneath the edge of the layer of birch bark. Close to the point of the chin of the displaced mandible was a barrel-shaped glass bead, ivory-colored (Pl. XXVI, R; Pl. XXV, Fig. 3C, No. 21789). Within .1 foot were one-half of an elliptical bead (Pl. XXVI, P, No. 21788) and 2 beads of the same type but split in two longitudinally, all with orange and white stripes (Pl. XXV, Fig. 3D, No. 21792). Another bead of the same type, broken in half transversely, adhered to the skull after its removal from the grave (No. 21790). Near the west end of the grave were a small piece of fabric and 2 small flint flakes (No. 21786).

Grave 14. Depth, .9 foot; length, 3.3 feet; width, 2.9 feet. There was no burial.

Grave 15 (Pl. XV, Fig. 2). Depth, 1.65 feet; length, 2.7 feet; width, 2.2 feet; depth of fill, 1.1 feet. This grave contained the disarticulated remains of 3 individuals, and the cremated remains of another (barring the possibility that they did not represent the missing bones of the disarticulated burials). The 2 bundle burials comprised 2 sets of long bones lying parallel in an east-west direction on opposite sides of the grave and with skulls present in both cases. Skull A (Fig. 5) lay at the

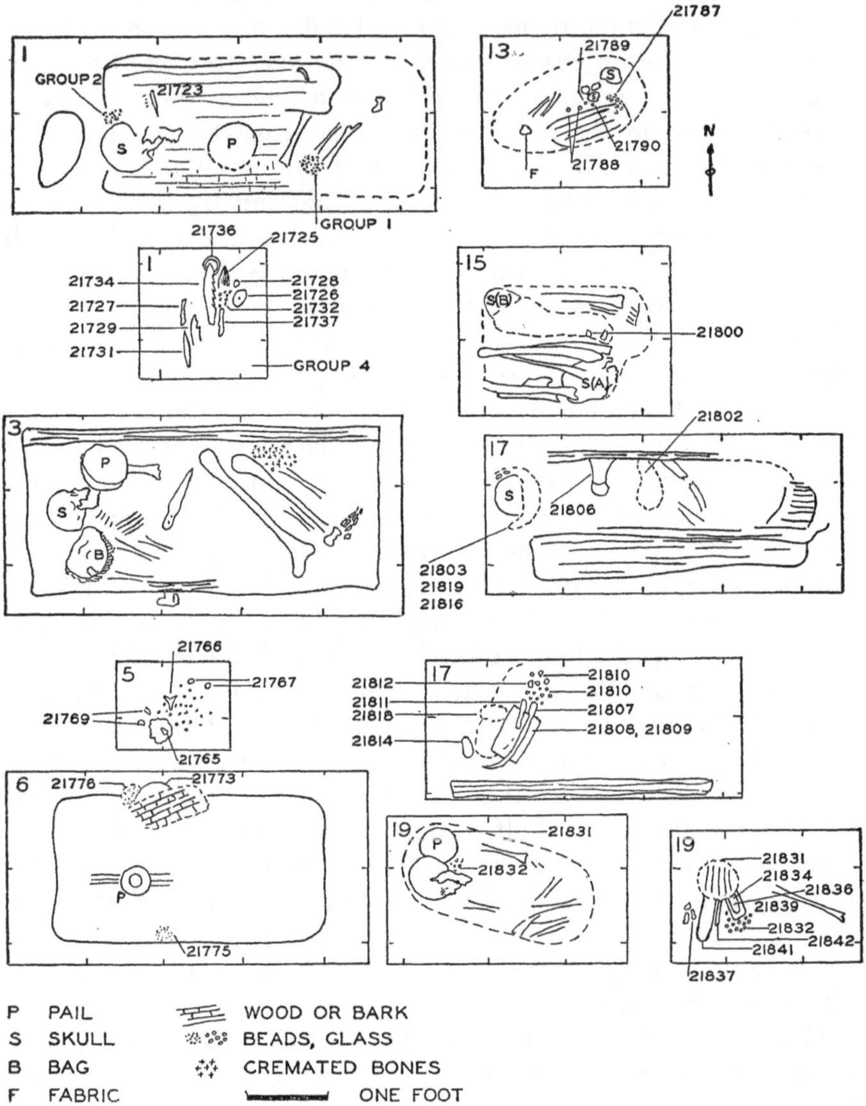

FIG. 5. Burials and artifacts. Graves 1, 3, 5, 6, 13, 15, 17, and 19.

east end of the group on the south side; Skull B at the west end of the group to the north. Skull A lay on the left side, facing slightly north of east; this and its complementary bones are those of an individual of 19 or 20 years of age. Skull B lay on the right side facing east, and the left half is missing. Skull B and its complementary bones are those of a child aged 5 to 8 years. The mandible of Skull A was disarticulated, lying on one side, to the south, at the west end of the long bones, 1.7 feet from its proper position if articulated with the skull. The mandible of Skull B was in articulation.

Immediately to the north of the bundle burial of Skull A were 9 long bones of a child of 1 to 4 years of age.

The cremated remains were in an area 1.4 feet long and .5 foot in greatest width, partly covering Skull B and the long bones of the infant adjoining the bundle burial to the south. A small strip of birch bark lay at the east end of the long bones of the bundle burial to the north.

Artifacts. One small discoidal white glass bead, as in Plate XXV, Figure 2D (No. 21798), adhered to the occiput of Skull B. Lying on the upper surface of the cremated bone fragments, at the east end, were 3 irregular lumps of glass (No. 21800) formed by the partial or complete melting and consequent fusing of glass beads. All 3 lumps have imbedded in them areas of white glass and, in one instance, of blue glass recognizable as beads which were not melted sufficiently to lose their shape entirely. Two of the lumps show as many as 7 beads in a row as if strung.

GRAVE 16 (Fig. 1). Depth, .6 foot; diameter, 3.0 feet. This depression was 2.0 feet northwest of Grave 15. In cross section it was rounded, unlike the unfilled hole of Grave 15, which was V-shaped. This grave contained no burial, but there was a quartzite flake at the north edge, .3 foot below the surface (No. 21801).

GRAVE 17. Depth, 1.8 feet; length, 4.5 feet; width, 1.7 feet; depth of fill, .8 foot. This was the first to be excavated of the graves of Group B (Fig. 2) and was on the second terrace above the lake. After the dead leaves and roots were cleared,

19 blocks of limestone or quartzite were revealed as intentionally placed around this grave, 16 of them around the outer edge of the earth thrown out of the grave and 3 in or on the sides of the unfilled hole. The flexed skeleton of an adult lay on the back, skull to west, facing east, legs closely flexed upward and inclining to the south. Pelvis, vertebral column, and arm and hand bones were missing, apparently completely disintegrated. Nearly vertical strips of bark were on the north, east, and south sides of the grave. The strip on the north side was 2.4 feet long and extended to within 1.3 feet of the east end. Its lower edge was at the bottom of the grave; this strip was .3 foot in greatest thickness, the top being at the level of the teeth of the mandible. The bark or wood at the east end began 1.0 foot from the top of the grave. The rotted fragments hung down the side, held together by roots. Pieces of bark or wood lay over the skeleton, and several parallel strips were inclined from a point near the top of the grave down to the level of the top of the skull, from the east end of the grave to the skull, but no farther. This inclined strip of bark or wood is interpreted as an original roof, covered with earth and 2 or 3 rocks, which had caved in. It was impossible to determine whether or not the pieces of bark over the skeleton were part of this roof. The skeleton lay in a deposit of loose black humus .2 foot thick.

Artifacts. Beads in considerable quantity were in 2 separate areas, both within the limits of the layer of black humus, in the abdominal region, and on the east side of the skull and beneath it (Fig. 5). In the abdominal region were 2228 discoidal medium-sized white beads (Pl. XXVI, B; Pl. XXV, Fig. 2C, No. 21802) and 3 tubular white beads (No. 21802) like that in Plate XXV, Figure 2A. In front of and beneath the skull were the following beads: 327 discoidal, small, white (No. 21803), of the type shown in Plate XXV, Figure 1G; 75 tubular white (No. 21803), of the type shown in Plate XXV, Figure 2A; 2984 tubular black (No. 21803), of the type shown in Plate XXV, Figure 1D, and 3 discoidal white (No. 21803) as in Plate XXV, Figure 2C. The following beads were beneath and in front of the skull: 909 discoidal, white, small (Pl. XXV, Fig. 1G, Nos.

21816, 21819, 21802); 90 tubular white (Pl. XXV, Fig. 2A, Nos. 21819, 21852); 2487 tubular black (Pl. XXV, Fig. 1D, No. 21819, 21852); 2 tubular blue (Pl. XXV, Fig. 1B, No. 21852). In front of the skull was a brass bangle (No. 21805).

On the north side of the grave was an iron axe, with its edge to the north, touching the strip of bark or wood along that side (Pl. XXI, F, No. 21806).

Directly beneath the skull was a small rectangular mirror, with other objects around, beneath, and over it. The mirror lay on a piece of bark or decayed wood, which in its outlines indicates that it was a frame with a handle (Pl. XXII, Fig. 1C). On the mirror was a curved iron knife similar to that in Plate XIX, Figure 1F, its point projecting beyond the edge of the mirror to the southwest. Beside this knife at its north end was a small iron spike with a wooden handle (No. 21811). Adjoining the northwest corner of the mirror was an oval iron strike-a-light (Pl. XIX, Fig. 1D, No. 21818); at the northeast end of the mirror were 167 lead shot and 12 musket balls of lead (No. 21810). There was 1 gunflint in this deposit of artifacts (Pl. XXIII, B, No. 21812), and also a flint for a strike-a-light (Pl. XXIII, E, No. 21817). The remainder consisted of a brass button (No. 21820) and brass bangles (Nos. 21815, 21813), some of the latter encased in or attached to pieces of skin with the hair or fur well preserved. A portion of skin around 4 brass bangles (No. 21814) contained 3 claws from the forefoot of an otter. The bangles are of the type shown in Plate XX, Figure 1C, D, and the type of brass button is shown in Plate XX, Figure 1B. A large iron knife lay parallel to and adjoining the south edge of the grave to the east of this deposit of artifacts (Pl. XIX, Fig. 2B, No. 21822). Two brass bangles (No. 21804) were within .2 foot of the left ear of the skull. One unworked piece of blue flint came from a depth of 1.0 foot in this grave (No. 21024).

The glass beads with this and the other burials were clearly deposited as parts of belts or necklaces, but postburial disturbances by roots had obliterated all original patterns.

GRAVE 18 (Pl. XVI, Fig. 2). Depth, 1.5 feet; length, 3.6 feet;

width, 1.7 feet; depth of fill, .8 foot. This grave contained at the west end a part of a left parietal bone, the petrous part of a temporal bone, and part of the mandible, permanent dentition unerupted, of a child of about 8 years of age; at the east end of the grave were pieces of foot bones. The skull probably faced to the north, lying on the left side. The age of the individual and the length of the grave suggest a flexion.

After the leaves and roots had been cleared, 20 large boulders, limestone for the most part with a few of quartzite, were at the surface of the ground, within the area occupied by the earth that had been thrown out. One boulder lay a little beyond this area to the north (Fig. 2). Two other boulders lay between Graves 18 and 19. The human remains and the accompanying artifacts were in a stratum of loose black humus .1 foot thick which covered the bottom of the grave and extended up the sides .3 foot.

Artifacts. A silver gorget lay .4 foot east of the mandible (Pl. XXII, Fig. 1B, No. 21826). On it is engraved a crown, beneath which are stamped the initials "R.C." (Pl. XXI, G; Fig. 6). At the other end of the grave, in the southeast corner, was a small brass pail upside down (No. 21827) and over the bones of the feet. Beneath the pail was a round iron strike-a-light (Pl. XIX, Fig. 1A, No. 21828), at the center of which was an irregular flint flake (No. 21829) which, because of this close and direct association, was certainly used with the strike-a-light.

Grave 19 (Pl. XV, Fig. 1). Depth, 1.5 feet; length, 2.4 feet; width, 1.2 feet; depth of fill, .3 foot. To the eye the fill was deeper than this, since the earth cast out from the grave had been kept (or gathered up) within the encircling boulders (Fig. 4). The arrangement of the boulders was more symmetrical around this grave than around any of the others (Fig. 2). There were 14 boulders, chiefly of limestone, in an oval line and 1 offset from this line at the northwest end. The open hole at the center directly over the burial was smaller than usual. The burial was that of a child of about 8 years of age, lying on the back, head slightly to the north of west, facing south, flexed, with the knees elevated and leaning to the south. The lower arm bones lay across the abdomen, but the bones of the hands were missing. A stratum of loose black humus, .1 foot thick, covered the bottom of the grave. Several strips of bark or wood, chemically preserved, were beneath the brass pail. These may have been part of a bark covering for the burial.

Artifacts. These were all in a single group at and beneath the skull (Fig. 5). Adjoining the skull on the north was a small crudely fashioned brass pail without a handle, lying right side up (Pl. XVII, Fig. 1B, No. 21831). The area occupied by the deposit lay beneath both the skull and the pail. Under the mandible and extending toward the brass pail were 206 blue tubular glass beads of the type shown in Plate XXV, Figure 1B. A rectangular iron strike-a-light (Pl. XIX, Fig. 1C, No. 21839) contained a piece of worked flint to be used with it (Pl. XXIII, C, No. 21834) and a quartzite flake (No. 21836). A large iron knife lay with its wooden handle beneath the occiput and the blade beneath the brass pail (Pl. XIX, Fig. 2A, No. 21841). Parallel and immediately east was an iron awl with a wooden handle which lay to the north (No. 21842). Under the strike-a-light were a small piece of needle-like iron rod (No. 21843), a lump of red ochre about 1 cubic centimeter in size (No. 21846), and a beadlike section of bird bone with one end cut (No. 21844). Among the beads was a small piece of iron of indeterminate shape (No. 21840); beneath the south end of the strike-a-light was a coinlike disk of lead (Pl. XX, Fig. 1A, No. 21845). Under the central part of the iron knife was a small strip of bark with holes in it (No. 21838). Pieces of a mussel shell (No. 21837) were .1 foot west of the wooden handle of the iron knife. One piece of fabric (No. 21833) lay near the center of the deposit of artifacts, and a small fragment of wood (No. 21835), which may have served as tinder, adjoined the strike-a-light on the west.

Grave 20. Depth, 1.8 feet; length, 3.9 feet; width, 3.1 feet; depth of fill, .8 foot. There was no burial. At the bottom of the hole, beneath 1.0 foot of earth, was a flat stone rectangular in outline, 1.0 foot across and .6 foot thick. It bore no artificial alterations of any kind.

ARTIFACTS

The chief value of an early historic site is the association in closed deposits, such as graves and pits, of both native and European materials. It is by this means that their contemporaneity is established and that dates can be given for native objects. Through material of this type the cultural connections of early historic sites are established, though identification of their occupants with historically known Indian groups is a matter of actual written records from the period.

NATIVE ARTIFACTS

The 43 native artifacts from Old Birch Island are of 5 materials: stone, clay, bone or antler, wood, and shell, counting unworked flakes as artifacts. They were distributed among 13 graves in amounts of 1, 2, 3, 6, and 10 items, with the largest number in Graves 1 and 8, though in the latter all 10 were of the same type. The graves with the most native objects were not those with the most European objects, even if a group of the small glass beads was counted as a single artifact, that is, as a belt, but Grave 1 had 10 native articles and 8 items of European make.

Stone. The 21 stone artifacts include pieces of flint and 1 piece of quartzite, these being simply flakes or thicker pieces bearing flake scars. The presence of cortex on one of the thicker pieces from Grave 12 indicates a naturally eroded pebble as the source. None of these specimens has features distinctive enough to describe in detail, and none can be identified as a by-product in the making of any of the flint artifacts. The flake (No. 21829) which lay within the annular strike-a-light in Grave 18 is no more than 2 mm. thick and 2 cm. long. On 2 edges indentations were made in striking off sparks to produce fire. Small flake scars border these edges on the outer flake surface. The striking platform has an angle of a little less than 90 degrees, and the detachment fracture is of the hinge type.

Of the 6 pieces of flint that resemble end scrapers, 2 were probably for use with strike-a-lights. One of these (Pl. XXIII, C,

No. 21834) lay inside of the ring formed by an iron strike-a-light in Grave 19, with a piece of quartzite (No. 21836). The other (Pl. XXIII, E, No. 21817) lay beneath the skull in Grave 17. Both specimens are keeled along one side, but the irregularity of the outlines and the associations suggest the chipping of shallow notches by striking sparks. The other 4 lack such notches and are steeply keeled with symmetrical outlines. One is nearly square (Pl. XXIII, B, No. 21812), and its position in Grave 17 among a number of lead musket balls makes it almost certain that the specimen is a gunflint. The other 3 (Pl. XXIII, A, D, F, Nos. 21751, 21747, 21728, respectively) are of 3 different colors and were probably also used as gunflints. The flint from Grave 3 (Pl. XXIII, D, No. 21747) appears to have been burnt on the keeled surface, which is blackened.

Two elongated pieces of stone were found, one with a burial. The other, which was on the surface of the ground, is a bar of slate roughly pecked into an oval cross section (Pl. XXII, Fig. 2F, No. 21847). It lay under leaf mold 5 feet north of Grave 3, 2.5 feet from the edge of the bluff. The greatest thickness is 3 cm.; the length is 18.5 cm. One side is smooth, as if it had been ground. The water-worn sandstone pebble (Pl. XXII, Fig. 2B, No. 21749) from Grave 3 is unworked. Its surface is pitted by leaching of softer or less cemented areas, perhaps as the result of use as a whetstone, since what is left of the original surface is blackened. The stone awl or punch from Grave 1 (Pl. XXII, Fig. 2D, No. 21723) is limestone, 8 mm. thick and with a square cross section. A strip of brass of about the same width lay beneath it.

The projectile point from the site was 3 feet south of the center of Grave 10, which contained no burial (Pl. XXIII, G, No. 21782). Its greatest thickness is about 5 mm.; length, 4.3 cm. The material is gray flint or chert, with an outer reddishness which has a depositional origin, since it can be removed with water. The coloring is almost certainly red ochre. The tip of this specimen was missing.

An incised red sandstone disk was in Grave 1 (Pl. XXI, C, D, No. 21726). On one side are 2 concentric circles enclosing an

8-pointed star, the center of which is the hole through the middle of the disk. Around the rim, outside of the outer of the 2 circles, is another formed by 36 dots or circular holes, about 1 mm. in diameter and 1 mm. to .5 mm. in depth. The 2 concentric circles are rather crudely incised, the inner being slightly deeper than the outer. The lines of the star are shallower still, some being difficult to see except when held slanting to the light.

The reverse side of the disk (Pl. XXI, D) has 10 incised straight radial lines and 6 radial lines of dots of the same character as the circle of 36 dots on the opposite side of the disk. Four of these dotted radial lines have 6 dots each, 1 has 7, and 1 has 5. The complete design on this face is that of 4 triangles enclosing plain surfaces and 6 triangles enclosing 1 radial dotted line each. Two sets each of the latter type of triangle adjoin each other, and the other 2 triangles of this type are adjoined by triangles enclosing plain surfaces. At the apex of 1 of the triangles enclosing a plain surface is a single dot, 1 mm. from the central hole through the disk, indicating apparently that a dotted radial line was started in this triangle by mistake and discontinued. The radial lines are .1 mm. to about .5 mm. in depth and of an average width of about .7 mm. The disk is 7.5 mm. thick at center; it does not vary 1 mm. from a diameter of 4 cm. The cross section is lens-shaped. The central hole is 5 mm. in diameter, and its sides are parallel, that is, it is not of the countersunk type.

The biconical specimen of black stone from Grave 1 (Pl. XXII, Fig. 2A, No. 21725) is 12.1 cm. long, 2.2 cm. in one diameter and 3.2 cm. in the other. Facets produced by grinding are observable in slanting light.

Clay. The human-effigy tobacco pipe from Grave 3 (Pl. XXI, A, B, No. 21750) is made of very fine-grained, untempered clay. The hole for the stem is 9 mm. in diameter, and the mouth of the bowl 18 mm. across. The total height is 7.4 cm. The base has a projecting ridge in the same plane as the stem hole, 8 mm. wide, 5 mm. thick, and as long as the base of the pipe. At the center is a transverse hole 3 mm. in diameter. The arms are depicted in low relief, and the right arm is missing. It appears to have been detached during the carving of the pipe in an attempt to undercut the arm to bring it free in its central part from the body. On the left hand the fingers are not represented, but 2 low ridges extending from the shoulders to a central point at the base of the neck represent either the collar bones or a feature of attire. The middle line of the neck in front is also a ridge, which meets the other 2 ridges at their junction. The bowl is conical in cross section and 38 mm. deep. In the front, from the shoulder to a point level with the lower margin of the stem hole, are 7 long, carelessly incised lines, with a few very indistinct lines in a transverse direction suggesting a wide crosshatch over the entire area.

The catlinite object from Grave 5 (Pl. XX, Fig. 1E, No. 21766) has a maximum thickness of 1.5 mm. A hole .9 mm. in diameter extends from the tip to the apex of the indented base. This piece is apparently a bead, as it was found among many glass beads (Fig. 5).

Bone and Antler. Bone and antler objects from the site are few. The awl or skewer from Grave 2 (Pl. XVIII, Fig. 2 A, No. 21744) is slightly bowed and may have been made from the rib of a deer or bear. The surface is much pitted by leaching or the activities of small organisms. The cross section is thinly oval, with an average thickness, below the knobbed end, of about 5 mm. The 4 harpoons from Grave 1 (Pl. XVIII, Fig. 2) indicate a type that is barbed only on 1 side. Two, B and E, (Nos. 21729, 21734, respectively) have small holes near the bases, but this feature is not present in C (No. 21730). The fourth harpoon (No. 21729) is a fragment of the midsection of one of the same type as the rest. The end of a barb of B has been broken off, making it appear to be square. The transverse cross sections of all of these specimens except E are symmetrical, being represented by an oval which is pointed at one end and straight at the end which bears the barbs. Consequently, the side opposite the barbs is a narrow ridge. Specimen E is thinner, concavo-convex in cross section, the concave face showing in the illustration. All of these harpoons are of antler with the possible exception of this one, which may have been made of a rib of a large mammal.

One small piece of bird leg bone (No. 21844), from Grave 19, may be part of a bead or the end of a leg bone which was left. One end of this piece is cut neatly across, but the other is ragged, thin walled, and unworked. The cross section is oval, 1 cm. by 8 mm.; length, 4.3 cm.

Shell. Of shell artifacts other than beads there is but 1 specimen, the ladle from Grave 3 (Pl. XVIII, Fig. 1B, No. 21760). It is made from the carapace of the painted turtle (*Chrysemys picta marginata*). The bowl of the ladle has a depth of 11 mm. below the sides, at the central point, and the over-all longitudinal curve has a maximum convexity of 2 cm. The edges are about 1 mm. thick except at the hafted end, where a cut bevel forms a knife edge. This end has a small hole centrally placed with reference to the lateral edges.

Ten beads carved from the central column of a large marine shell were in Grave 8 (Pl. XX, Fig. 2, No. 21780). They are tubular and 3.5 cm. to 1.5 cm. in length. The surfaces of 6 are more or less grooved and pitted, and the edges of the lamina are revealed. This is apparently due to the leaching of the softer calcareous substances.

Wood. The wooden objects, though perhaps reflecting the forms of European metal utensils, may be regarded as native, since they could have been made by those who buried their dead in this cemetery. These comprise a small bowl, a tray, a large ladle, and a thin piece of wood probably part of the bowl of a spoon (No. 21772). The bowl (No. 21777) is the only complete and undamaged specimen (Pl. XVII, Fig. 2B). It is 8 cm. long, 5.5 cm. wide, and 2.5 cm. deep at center inside. At each end the lip or rim is raised 6 mm. above the general level, forming scallop-like handles 16 mm. wide at the base. The lip is flat, nearly 2 mm. in width. The base is slightly rounded, and a ridge separates it from the insloping sides.

The tray was originally about 13 cm. long (Pl. XVII, Fig. 3B, No. 21720). The depth, within an inch of one end, is 3 cm. The edges are missing or broken, but the depth at the center of the tray was probably not more than 3.5 cm. The back and sides have 5 ridges which delimit 6 slightly concave longitudinal areas. The ridges stand not more than 4 mm. above the bottoms of the areas they delimit. A vertical ridge is also at the middle of the end of the tray.

Part of the wooden ladle is also missing, but the general outline of the entire piece is indicated. The handle was probably continuous with the bowl and not separately fastened. The deepest part of the bowl is 1 cm. below the sides, and the lip, or edge, is about .15 mm. thick (Pl. XVII, Fig. 3A, No. 21759). The thin curved piece of wood from Grave 6 (No. 21772) has the appearance of part of the bowl of a spoon or ladle. The curved edge is a cut one and is .8 mm. thick, the thickness increasing inward from the edge. The material is wood rather than bark, and probably maple or birch (Pl. XVIII, Fig. 1C).

A piece of birch bark from Grave 19 (No. 21838) with a maximum width of 2 cm. has 3 small holes in a transverse line, spaced 3 mm. apart, the line being 2 mm. from the end which is a cut edge. This band of bark is curved around three-quarters of a circle about the size of the tip of the little finger.

The mirror in Grave 17 (Pl. XXII, Fig. 1C) had a frame of wood. The glass is 9 cm. by 5.5 cm. The frame, which lay beneath the glass when found, is in an advanced state of decay and is bowed longitudinally. It appears to have been a piece of wood not more than about 7 mm. thick, and 1 face was gouged or chiseled out for the insetting of the glass. The outer surface of the glass was apparently flush with the sides of the chiseled areas, so that the glass itself was held in a frame, the side ridges of which were about 2 mm. wide. At the top of the mirror the unchiseled part of the frame extended about one-half inch beyond the edge of the glass. At the other end there was probably a handle, as the wood extends an inch beyond the edge of the glass, terminating in a ragged broken edge. The surface of this area inset for the glass is almost completely covered with a thin layer, cracked and pitted, of shiny light brown to gray material of the consistency of a dried coat of paint. Although none adheres to the glass, this material gave it the capacity for reflecting an image. The glass is 1.3 mm. thick.

TRADE MATERIALS

The trade materials represent the workmanship and influence of Europeans, and they date this cemetery as post-Columbian. It is to be presumed that all of them were made by Europeans, either in the centers of early historic industry in northeastern North America or in Europe. Those of metal, with the exception of the silver and some of the brass objects, are distinctly utilitarian and are chiefly of iron.

Metal. Four of these items are knives. One (No. 21735) is the central part of a blade, and the other 3 are complete enough to indicate a variation in length between 17 cm. and 25 cm. In these 3 specimens the part occupied by the handle is narrow, so that a shoulder marks the dividing point between this part and the cutting edge. These 3 knives originally had wooden handles, parts of which adhere to the metal. The presence of rivets on 2 (Pl. XIX, Fig. 2B, C, Nos. 21822, 21754, respectively) indicates the way in which the 2 wooden slabs forming the handles were attached. On the other complete knife there are no rivets. This one (Pl. XIX, Fig. 2A, No. 21841) is distinguished by the absence of a point on the blade. The end is broadly curved and, unless the point was broken off, suggests an exclusively culinary use. The sharp ends of the other 2 would allow a more adventurous use in warfare and hunting.

Two knives, curved longitudinally near the ends (Pl. XIX, Fig. 1F, No. 21738), are probably carving tools and are especially adapted to making wooden receptacles and ladles of the type already described. The knife illustrated has a triangular cross section, with the apex of the triangle forming a ridge which greatly strengthened the implement on its concave face. The other is simply a thin flat strip of iron. It is not apparent that the specimen illustrated had a wooden handle, but part of such a handle, now badly rotted, remains on one side of the proximal third of the other. This part of the blade of this knife is about 4 mm. wider than the rest and at the proximal end is turned abruptly at a right angle, forming a short hook the only function of which would seem to have been to hold the handle more firmly. There is no indication that the handle was fastened with rivets.

The 2 iron axes (Pl. XXI, E, F,) Nos. 21753, 21806, respectively) from Graves 3 and 17, are common types for the period. One is 1.9 cm. shorter than the other, but otherwise they differ little. The hafting hole is elliptical in both, coming to a point on the side toward the blade. The curved chisel from Grave 1 (Pl. XIX, Fig. 1G, No. 21737) has a socket for insertion of the handle. It is possible that this implement was used as a gouge in hollowing pieces of wood in the making of bowls and similar utensils. It is curved to a distance of 5 cm. from the sharp edge, like the underside of a spoon, but it is not cupped on the upper side. The curve is on the long axis, and its purpose was to obtain leverage on the material undercut at the edge. The 4 awl-like specimens have other differences than those of dimension. One (Pl. XIX, Fig. 1E, No. 21731) has a triangular cross section. This is the longest of the 4, and it apparently had a handle of wood. The point was probably conical in contrast to that from Grave 17 (No. 21811), which appears to have been more like the edge of a chisel. The other end of this specimen is beveled on 2 sides, but the end proper is blunt and about 1 mm. wide. This end was set into the wooden handle, part of which is present. The complete handle was round, about 1.5 cm. in diameter, and at least 4.5 cm. long. The metal part was set into it a distance of 1.4 cm. The awl from Grave 19 (No. 21842) is too much rusted to reveal anything of the original character of its point, but parts of a wooden handle are still present. The other specimen from Grave 19 (No. 21843) is the smallest of the 4, and nothing indicates that it had a handle or that it was eyed as a needle.

Other iron objects are the cylinder (No. 21763) from Grave 4, which may have been part of a gun barrel or perhaps a ferrule of some sort; a V-shaped specimen 9 mm. by 8 mm., 1.5 mm. thick (No. 21840); and a button (No. 21820). The strike-a-lights are of closed and open types. The 2 closed specimens (Pl. XIX, Fig. 1A, D, Nos. 21828, 21818, respectively) are alike in that the edges of the band of metal form the outer and inner borders of the implements; one is oval and long, to fit over the 4 fingers of the hand, and the other is small and round. One of the open specimens (Pl. XIX, Fig. 1C, No. 21839) is built in the same way, although it is rectangular and the 2 ends of the open side are curled outward. On the other open specimen (Pl. XIX, Fig. 1B, No. 21736) the faces of the band of metal form the outer and inner surfaces of the oval implement. What is apparently an iron button was found in Grave 17 (No. 21820). It is in badly corroded halves, and a peglike projection from the inner side of one of the halves suggests the manner in which they were fastened together. Possibly the peg was threaded, but this is not indicated. The other half has a similar projection from the inner side, though corrosion has destroyed its form. It is possible that 2 separate buttons are represented.

The 41 brass objects include 5 pails, 2 buttons, 23 bangles, 1 spoon, and 2 small strips of sheet brass. All but 1 of the pails are well made, with rolled-over rims, and they were apparently in good condition when deposited in the graves. The poorly made pail (Pl. XVII, Fig. 1B, No. 21831) from Grave 19 is like 3 of the others in general outline, but the rim is not rolled, and the lack of that strengthening feature has allowed the body to become bent and warped. The bail, or handle, is missing, but like those of the other pails it was fastened to iron strips riveted to the sides. Only 1 of these is present. Of the other 3 pails of this general type the sides pass into the bottom in a curve on 2 (Nos. 21719, 21758), while on the other there is a sharp angle (Pl. XVII, Fig. 1A, No. 21827). These 3 pails have iron handles, looped into brass lugs fastened to the sides with brass rivets. This is the case also with the smaller pail from Grave 6 (Pl. XVII, Fig. 2A, No. 21774), which is the only pail having a constricted neck.

The brass spoon (Pl. XVIII, Fig. 1A, No. 21746) was the first object found in this cemetery. It was brought up when the leaf mold covering Grave 3 was removed in an effort to determine whether or not the depression was natural or artificial. There was nothing to indicate that a handle had been attached to it, and more careful removal of the remaining leaf mold later on revealed nothing that could be identified as the rotted remains of a wooden or bone handle. The bowl of this spoon is about 6 cm. long, and it merges without a break into a narrowing backward part which rises above the level of the top of the bowl proper. This part is for the attachment of a handle, since it is perforated 2.5 cm. from the tip, but the spoon would be usable without such a handle. The perforation is 4 mm. in diameter, and between it and the tip this part lies in about the same plane as that of the top of the bowl proper. This is probably the proper position, since a wooden handle fastened at that angle would be in a correct position for use as a spoon. The bowl has a depth of 9 mm.

The bangles are simple conical sheets of brass bent around so that one edge meets the other (Pl. XX, Fig. 1C, D). They range in length from 1.5 cm. to 2.5 cm. One of the 2 small strips of brass from Grave 1 (Pl. XXII, Fig. 2C, No. 21723) lay on the object which has been described as a stone punch. It is about the same width as the punch, but only two-thirds as long. There is no indication that the strip of brass was fastened to the implement. The other piece of brass is a little longer and wider (Pl. XXII, Fig. 2E, No. 21727). Its edges are ragged in places, and there are irregular indentations in the surface. The 2 brass buttons from Grave 5 (Pl. XX, Fig. 1B, No. 21767) are elliptical in transverse cross section, 1 cm. thick, and each is made of 2 equal castings, one of which has a loop for fastening the button to the garment. The loop is cast in 1 piece with the rest of the hemisphere. The whole button thus made is hollow, and the upper half (or outer half, as worn) bears concentric circular grooves as ornamentation.

The largest of the several lead (or pewter) objects from the site is the circular disk or gorget from Grave 6 (Pl. XXII, Fig. 1A, No. 21773). It is saucer-shaped and 1.6 cm. deep. On 1 side of the center are 2 perforations, 3 mm. in diameter and

4.7 cm. apart. The coinlike piece of lead from Grave 19 (Pl. XX, Fig. 1A, No. 21845) is 2 mm. thick. Unevenness of the 2 surfaces indicates that it was pounded into shape rather than cast. The piece may be an unfinished pendant. The outline departs from the circular for a short distance, where it comes to a low rounded point.

Of the lead musket balls from Grave 17 (No. 21810) all are spherical and in original condition except 1, which obviously has been shot and retrieved. It is flattened on 1 side, the di-

FIG. 6. Crown engraved on silver crescent from Grave 18 (No. 21826); see also Plates XXI, G, and XXII, Fig. 1B. Scale, twice actual size.

ameter is 5 mm. greater than that of the intact specimens, and there are deep grooves in the sides and faces. The greatest thickness is 1 cm., whereas the diameter of the other is 1.5 cm. The 167 lead shot from Grave 17 (No. 21810) are all intact. Their diameters vary from .35 cm. to .5 cm.

The only object of silver from this cemetery is the crescent found with the burial in Grave 18 (Pl. XXII, Fig. 1B, No. 21826). On the front of this piece is engraved a crown, an enlarged drawing of which is shown in Figure 6. Just beneath the crown is the imprint of the initials of the maker of the gorget, Robert Cruikshanks[25] (see Pl. XXI, G).

Cloth. Of the 2 samples of cloth from the site one is a fragment adhering to a bone from Grave 1 and the other is a bag from Grave 3 (Pl. XI, Fig. 2, No. 21757). The bag was evidently of leather-lined cloth. All that remains is the mouth of the cloth bag, a strip of woven material 1 to 3 cm. wide, ragged on the lower border, and about one-third of the same part of the interior leather bag, a strip of leather about 5 cm. wide with the lower border ragged. The cloth part consists of 2 strands, the inner having its 2 ends tied together in a large double square knot. The cloth is folded over at the mouth of the bag, doubled back downward 5 mm., and though it appears to have been folded or woven around a circular stiffening splint, there is no such feature. The cloth is stiff, and at the fold there is an effect of a slight outrolling of the lip of the bag rather than a sharply distinguished edge. The mouth of the cloth part has a diameter of approximately 19 cm. The weave is that of a plain plaiting in which the weft for the most part is carried over 2 of the warp elements at a time, but occasionally over only 1, to hold the warp elements at their proper distances from one another. The weft strands are about .5 mm. in diameter and the warp about twice that size on the average. Both are twisted. The fabric is green, except for some parts of the warp, which are light brown, and is quite stiff, although it does not seem to have been brought to this green and stiff condition by any proximity in the grave to brass or other metal. The leather is 6 mm. thick. About 1.25 inches below the top or mouth there is a flaring shoulder which projects outward 1 inch beyond the base of the neck. The strands of cloth occupy the neck area only, and while the shoulder may be merely a preserved accidental bend in the leather as it lay in the grave beneath the weight of the earth, it is possible that this container was a leather jug with a capacity of a gallon or more. The leather is thick enough to have retained such a shape during use.

Beads. The glass beads are of 2 main types, monochrome and

[25] Quimby, 1936, p. 21.

polychrome. Beads from the early historic cemetery at Great Cloche Island are included in this discussion, since that site was but 3 miles from Old Birch Island, and there is not enough historic material from it to warrant a separate report. None of the beads from either site is of clear transparent glass. Of the 12569 beads only 71 are from Great Cloche Island, and only 17, from both sites, are polychrome. The monochrome beads are of 4 main colors: white, blue, black, and yellow (Pl. XXVI). Only 1 was yellow, and it came from Great Cloche Island.

Among the white beads there is some small variation in the shade, a good many being a pearly gray, but the difference is slight. Most of the 691 blue beads are dark blue, but 5 are of a lighter shade. They are all from Great Cloche Island. Monochrome beads are discoidal or tubular, with a great many on the borderline between. This 2-fold classification is, therefore, to some extent arbitrary, but the range in variation from one type to another in a given group of beads occurring together within a specific area is so small and consistent as to leave no doubt that a single impression as to size was either intentional or was prescribed by the conditions of trade. For example, on the abdomen of the skeleton in Grave 17 was a group of white beads, indicated on a plan of this grave in Figure 5 by No. 21802. The great majority of the 2228 beads from this area are somewhat larger than most of the white discoidal beads listed in the tabulation as "small" (I*a*, 1). None or very few of the largest beads in the latter class are as large as the smallest beads in this group in Grave 17. The differences in dimension are both in thickness and in diameter.

In the terminology applied to the shapes of the beads, "diameter" will be used in the same sense for both discoidal and tubular types, as signifying the distance between the edges of the bead in a line which is at a right angle to its hole. But "long" and "length" are used only in application to the tubular beads, as describing the greatest distance between the edges of the bead in a line parallel to its hole. For this dimension in describing the discoidal beads the words "thick" and "thickness" are used.

The several shapes of the monochrome beads are illustrated in Figure 7. No. 3 of the discoidal type differs from Nos. 1 and 2 in that the sides are straight rather than rounded. Despite the possession of this feature of the tubular type it is classed as discoidal because that term better describes its appearance (Pl. XXV, Fig. 1C). The tubular beads are almost all twice or more as long as the discoidal beads are thick. Two types are distinguished on the basis of the character of the corners of the outer contour. As is shown in Figure 7 one type has rounded, the other angular corners. The difference is due to the process of manufacture. Those with angular corners were cut sections of a small hollow rod of glass.[26] The ends of this type of bead are accordingly uneven, and the corners and edges are sharp. A hollow tube of blue glass made for this purpose was found with an early historic burial in Charlestown, Rhode Island, some years ago.[27] The beads with rounded corners were each made separately, and on the basis of this feature all of the discoidal beads, and 206 of the 5879 tubular beads, are alike. These 206 beads are all blue and came from Grave 19.

In the tabulation of beads (pp. 53–55) the distinction "tubular" is more satisfactory than "discoidal." Among tubular types there are none that can be described under the other term, but among the discoidal beads there are a few that might well be called tubular, because their sides are straight as in No. 3 (Fig. 7) and because they are a little thicker than the others. It is evidently a variation in dimension among them that is responsible for the change in form. In the thin beads the sides are formed by the corners; that is, there are no sides, only the conjoined rounded corners. There are no beads of the proportions of No. 1 (Fig. 7) with straight sides, but for many of the beads whose diameters are a little less and the thickness a little more, the sides become straight, though the corners remain rounded. Thus, among the 6671 beads classed as discoidal, white, and small there is a group from Grave 17 (No. 21803) in which the beads are of 2 different shapes: one from 1.3 mm. thick and 2 mm. in diameter to 2 mm. thick and 3 mm. in di-

[26] Beck, 1928, p. 60. [27] Anonymous, 1922, p. 18; pl. opp. p. 24.

ameter, with sides rounded, and corresponding to Nos. 1 or 2 (Fig. 7), and the other from 2.1 mm. thick and 1.9 mm. in diameter to 2.8 mm. thick and 2 mm. in diameter, with straight sides but rounded corners. This type corresponds to No. 3 (Fig. 7), but in the smaller ones the diameter is less, giving a more tubular appearance. In the lot of beads from Grave 17, 159 are of the straight-sided type and 168 have the sides rounded. Three are larger and are classed as medium-sized.

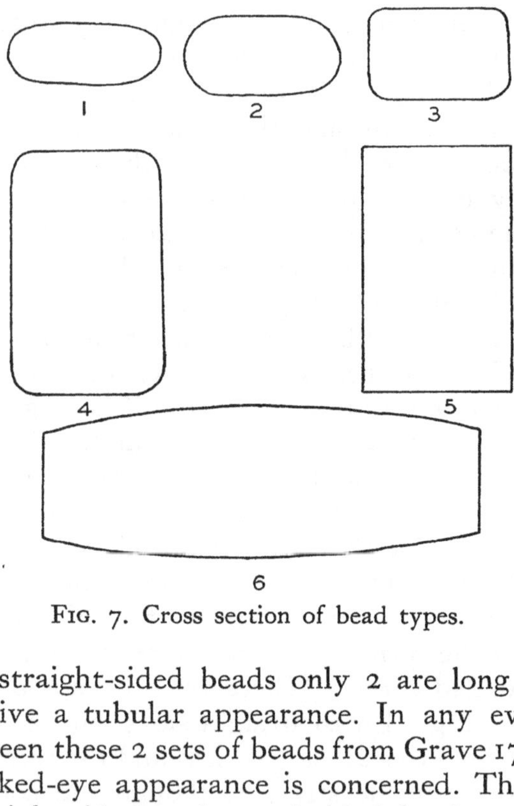

FIG. 7. Cross section of bead types.

Of the 159 straight-sided beads only 2 are long and narrow enough to give a tubular appearance. In any event the difference between these 2 sets of beads from Grave 17 is negligible so far as naked-eye appearance is concerned. The proportion between straight-sided and round-sided beads appears to be about the same in the other large lots of small white discoidal beads.

There are 5 lots of medium-sized white discoidal beads (I, *a*2) and the same 2 types, distinguished by roundness or straightness of the sides, are present. These beads average nearly twice as large as the small beads. Those with rounded sides range from 3 to 4.0 mm. in diameter and are from 2 to 3.0 mm. thick. The other type varies from 2.7 to 3 mm. in diameter and 2.5 to 4 mm. in thickness (Pl. XXV, Fig. 2C). The latter dimension, however, is an extreme case. The bead with that thickness is from Grave 17 (No. 21802). The average thickness is about 3.0 mm.

The large white discoidal beads are 5 to 6 mm. in diameter and 4.3 to 5 mm. in thickness. All of the 47 beads in this division have rounded sides and are of the proportions of No. 3 (Fig. 7) and of A in Plate XXV, Figure 3.

Of the 9 lots of blue discoidal beads, all from Old Birch Island are dark blue, and but 1 bead has enough thickness to give it the tubular appearance that so many of the white discoidal beads have. This bead is from Grave 5. It is 3.1 mm. in diameter and 3.0 mm. thick. For the rest, the range in diameter is 2.8 to 3.0 mm. Three or 4 beads have a diameter of about 3.8 mm., but they also depart from the others in form, being oval, with the other diameter much less. These were probably hastily made and are defective in comparison to the rest. The thickness of the blue discoidal beads from Old Birch Island ranges from 1.5 to 2 mm.

The blue beads from Great Cloche Island are of 3 shades, mostly different from the dark blue of Old Birch Island. Two (No. 21703) are greenish blue, 3 mm. thick and 3 mm. in diameter. One is light purple, 3.8 mm. thick, 2.8 mm. in diameter, and slightly tubular in appearance. Five are of a light translucent blue (No. 21703). The diameters are 3.0 to 3.2 mm.; widths, 2.0 to 2.6 mm. One is a dark blue discoidal bead (No. 21701) and another, a dark blue tubular bead (No. 21701), is 4.0 mm. long and 2.5 mm. in diameter.

In the 6 lots of tubular white beads (II*a*) some are as small as those with rounded corners that are classed as discoidal, but the ends of these beads are irregular and sharp and were apparently made by breaking a long glass tube into small sections. The range in length for these 6 lots is from 3 to 6 mm.;

in diameter from 2.5 to 4 mm. The largest of these beads, from Grave 1 (No. 21732), is 4 mm. in diameter and 6 mm. long. Those from Great Cloche Island (No. 21703) are smaller than the average of all the beads from Old Birch Island except those from Grave 17 (No. 21802).

There are 3 lots of blue tubular beads from Old Birch Island, and all are the same shade of dark blue, identical as to shade with the discoidal blue beads from Graves 1 and 17. In the lot of blue tubular beads from Grave 19 (Pl. XXV, Fig. 1B, No. 21832) some are of the true tubular type, made by breaking a long glass tube in sections, and others have almost certainly been made by curling the molten glass around a wire, as their ends and corners are rounded. The proportions of the 2 are about 100 of the latter to 106 of the former. In dimensions these beads, taking both kinds together, vary from 3.1 to 5 mm. The 2 beads from Grave 17 (No. 21852) are nearer the small size, and the 1 blue bead from Great Cloche Island is 5 mm. long and 2.5 mm. in diameter. It is probably of the broken type (No. 21701). Another bead from Great Cloche Island is purple. It is 3.5 mm. long, 2.5 mm. in diameter (Pl. XXV, Fig. 1D, No. 21703). The 19 beads from Grave 1 (Pl. XXV, Fig. 1A, No. 21770) are all of very nearly the same size, varying from 7 to 8 mm. in length, with a uniform diameter of 3 mm. All appear to have been made by sectioning a long glass tube.

The following dimensions characterize the 5 lots of tubular black beads (Pl. XXV, Fig. 1D; Pl. XXVI, I): diameters, 2.3 to 3.3 mm.; lengths. 3.0 to 5.0 mm. There is no appreciable difference in these lots as to average proportions, and all are apparently of the sectioned type. All of the black tubular beads from Old Birch Island were in Grave 17.

But 1 of each type of monochrome bead remains to be discussed here. The yellow tubular bead (Pl. XXVI, M, No. 21705), the only bead of that color in the entire collection, is 3.0 mm. in diameter and 4 mm. long. Two beads are basically spheroidal, and both are slightly flattened spheres. The smaller is black and has a diameter, at a right angle to the hole, of 5.0 mm. The material is cinder-like, and the surface is slightly pitted and shiny, with an iridescent green visible as the bead is rotated under a hand lens (Pl. XXVI, S; Pl. XXV, Fig. 3B, No. 21704). The other (No. 21780) has a diameter of 1 cm., at a right angle to the hole. The hole is 2.8 mm. in diameter. The color is grayish blue and the material may be porcelain. The only 10-sided bead (Pl. XXVI, Q, No. 21780) is from Grave 8 and is very dark blue glass. The greatest diameter is 1 cm. The hole has a diameter of 4 mm., and the ridges separating the facets are blunt rather than sharp. Of the 2 barrel-shaped beads the one is white and the other ivory. The former (Pl. XXV, Fig. 2B, No. 21704) is 8 mm. long and 4.5 mm. in diameter at center. The ivory bead (Pl. XXV, Fig. 3C; Pl. XXVI, R, No. 21789) is 1.2 cm. long and .8 cm. in diameter at center. The hole is 2.5 mm. in diameter.

The polychrome beads are described in the Classification of Glass Beads.

Classification of Glass Beads

References to glass beads from Old Birch Island and Great Cloche Island (Plate XXV) are in terms of types, not of individual specimens. For example, the small, white, discoidal bead from Grave 15 is referred to D, Plate XXV, Figure 2 (No. 21798), but the actual specimen illustrated, while exactly of the same type, is from Grave 6 (No. 21775).

MONOCHROME

I. DISCOIDAL

a. White

1. Small

703	Grave 5	No. 21770	Pl. XXV, Fig. 2D; Pl. XXVI, C.
315	Grave 1 (Grp. 2)	No. 21722	Pl. XXV, Fig. 2D; Pl. XXVI, C.
24	Grave 1 (Grp. 2)	No. 21732	Pl. XXV, Fig. 2D; Pl. XXVI, C.
958	Grave 1 (Grp. 1)	No. 21733	Pl. XXV, Fig. 2D; Pl. XXVI, C.
102	Grave 5	No. 21771	Pl. XXV, Fig. 1G; Pl. XXVI, C.
177	Grave 6	No. 21775	Pl. XXV, Fig. 2D; Pl. XXVI, C.
280	Grave 6	No. 21776	Pl. XXV, Fig. 2D; Pl. XXVI, C.
1	Grave 15	No. 21798	Pl. XXV, Fig. 2D; Pl. XXVI, C.
100	Grave 15	No. 21800	Approx. 100 fused.
327	Grave 17	No. 21803	Pl. XXV, Fig. 2D; Pl. XXVI, C.
865	Grave 17	No. 21819	Pl. XXV, Fig. 2D; Pl. XXVI, C.
20	Grave 17	No. 21816	Pl. XXV, Fig. 2D; Pl. XXVI, C.

24 Grave 17 No. 21852 Pl. XXV, Fig. 2D; Pl. XXVI, C.
17 Gt. Cloche No. 21703 Pl. XXV, Fig. 2D; Pl. XXVI, C.
3 Gt. Cloche No. 21701 Pl. XXV, Fig. 2E; Pl. XXVI, C.
2 Grave 17 No. 21802 Pl. XXV, Fig. 2D; Pl. XXVI, C.

2. Medium
2228 Grave 17 No. 21802 Pl. XXV, Fig. 2C; Pl. XXVI, B.
3 Grave 17 No. 21803 Pl. XXV, Fig. 2C; Pl. XXVI, B.
1 Grave 17 No. 21819 Pl. XXV, Fig. 2C; Pl. XXVI, B.
2 Grave 6 No. 21775 Pl. XXV, Fig. 2C; Pl. XXVI, B.
29 Gt. Cloche No. 21701 Pl. XXV, Fig. 2E; Pl. XXVI, B.

3. Large
47 Grave 1 (Grp. 2) No. 21732 Pl. XXV, Fig. 3A; Pl. XXVI, E.

b. Blue

1. Small
436 Grave 6 No. 21775 Pl. XXV, Fig. 1F; Pl. XXVI, K.
8 Grave 6 No. 21776 Pl. XXV, Fig. 1F; Pl. XXVI, K.
2 Grave 1 (Grp. 1) No 21733 Pl. XXV, Fig. 1F; Pl. XXVI, K.
4 Grave 5 No. 21771 Pl. XXV, Fig. 1G; Pl. XXVI, K.
3 Grave 5 No. 21770 Pl. XXV, Fig. 1F; Pl. XXVI, K.
1 Gt. Cloche No. 21701 Pl. XXV, Fig. 1H; Pl. XXVI, L.
5 Gt. Cloche No. 21703 Pl. XXV, Fig. 1H (a little lighter than J, Pl. XXVI).
2 Gt. Cloche No. 21703 Pl. XXV, Fig. 1C; Pl. XXVI, J (a little darker, and opaque).
1 Grave 15 No. 21800 Fused with white beads of this number.

c. Black

1. Small
1 Grave 5 No. 21770 Pl. XXV, Fig. 2D.

II. TUBULAR

a. White
75 Grave 17 No. 21852 Pl. XXV, Fig. 2A; Pl. XXVI, A.
15 Grave 17 No. 21819 Pl. XXV, Fig. 2A; Pl. XXVI, A.
75 Grave 17 No. 21803 Pl. XXV, Fig. 1D; Pl. XXVI, A.
3 Grave 17 No. 21802 Pl. XXV, Fig. 2A; Pl. XXVI, A.
1 Grave 1 (Grp. 2) No. 21732 Pl. XXV, Fig. 2A; Pl. XXVI, A.
4 Gt. Cloche No. 21703 Pl. XXV, Fig. 1D; Pl. XXVI, A; Pl. XXV, Fig. 2A.

b. Blue
206 Grave 19 No. 21832 Pl. XXV, Fig. 1B; Pl. XXVI, H.
2 Grave 17 No. 21852 Pl. XXV, Fig. 1B; Pl. XXVI, H.
19 Grave 5 No. 21770 Pl. XXV, Fig. 1A; Pl. XXVI, G.
1 Gt. Cloche No. 21703 Pl. XXV, Fig. 1D; Pl. XXVI, J. Slightly purple.
1 Gt. Cloche No. 21701 Pl. XXV, Fig. 2A; Pl. XXVI, H.

c. Black
2984 Grave 17 No. 21803 Pl. XXV, Fig. 1D.
1681 Grave 17 No. 21852 Pl. XXV, Fig. 1D; Pl. XXVI, I.

806 Grave 17 No. 21819 Pl. XXV, Fig. 1D.
1 Gt. Cloche No. 21703 Pl. XXV, Fig. 1E.
4 Gt. Cloche No. 21701 Pl. XXV, Fig. 1A.

d. Yellow
1 Gt. Cloche No. 21705 Pl. XXVI, M.

III. SPHEROIDAL

a. Blue
1 Grave 8 No. 21780 Diam. 1 cm., at right angle to hole, which is 2.8 mm. in diam. Opaque grayish blue (Pl. XX, Fig. 1G).

b. Black
1 Gt. Cloche No. 21704 Pl. XXV, Fig. 3B; Pl. XXVI, S. Iridescent.

IV. TEN-SIDED

a. Blue
2 Grave 8 No. 21780 Greatest diam. 1 cm. Diam. of hole 4 mm. Very dark blue. Pl. XX, Fig. 1F, Pl. XXVI, Q.

V. BARREL-SHAPED

a. White
1 Gt. Cloche No. 21704 Pl. XXV, Fig. 2B; Pl. XXVI, F.

VI. ELLIPTICAL

a. Ivory
1 Grave 13 No. 21789 Pl. XXV, Fig. 3C; Pl. XXVI, R. 1.2 cm. long; 8 mm. in diam. at center. Hole 2.5 mm. in diam.

POLYCHROME

I. ELLIPTICAL

a. Blue and red
1 Grave 13 No. 21788 1.3 cm. long; 7.3 mm. in diam. Longitudinal red stripe on 3 sides set within narrow bands of lighter blue than the general color of the bead. In 2 longitudinal halves.
½ Grave 13 No. 21788 Half of a bead identical with the other of this number, Pl. XXVI, P.
1 Grave 13 No. 21792 Length, 1.5 cm.; diam. 7 mm. Identical in shape with No. 21788. Pl. XXV, Fig. 3D.
1 Grave 13 No. 21790 Length, 1.7 cm.; diam. 7 mm. Identical in shape with No. 21788. In 2 transverse halves.

II. DISCOIDAL

a. Blue and white
14 Grave 13 Nos. 21787, 21785. Translucent dark blue glass, star and crescent designs painted on both faces. Diam.: parallel to hole, 1.5 to 2 cm.; at right angle to hole, 1.5 to 1.7 cm. Thickness, 4 mm.; holes, 2 to 2.5 mm. in diam. Pl. XXIV, Figs. 1, 2; Pl. XXVI, N, O.
No. 21787 includes the beads in Figure 5 as to position.

INTERPRETATION

The identity of the group of Indians who buried their dead in Old Birch Island Cemetery and the period of the use of the cemetery are closely related questions. The matter of the age of the site has precedence over the other, since the same native groups were not in the area throughout early historic times. The only definite date is provided by the silver crescent bearing the initials of Robert Cruikshanks, its maker, and this date applies only to Grave 18, in which it was found. Cruikshanks was a silversmith who came to Boston from London about 1768, and it is a matter of record that silver ornaments were made by him for the Indians in 1779.[28] Grave 18 could not, therefore, have been made before the arrival of Cruikshanks in Boston. Although this rather late date cannot be extended to the entire site, it is consonant with the absence of native pottery, which in this general area had probably been replaced by the metal vessels of the French by the year 1750, if not before. The remainder of the trade objects are all of types which had been current among the Indians on the Atlantic seaboard since 1650 at the latest. Recent work by Mr. Kenneth E. Kidd[29] near Midland, Ontario, at the south end of Georgian Bay, has provided upper limits for the presence in the Georgian Bay area of iron knives, axes, and blue glass beads like those from Old Birch Island. These were used by the occupants of the Mission of Ste Marie I, which was begun in 1639 by the Jesuits and abandoned in 1649.[30]

If the absence of native Indian pottery from Old Birch Island argues against a date before 1750, the presence of stone implements and cremation of the dead goes far to rule out anything after 1800. Cremation is of special significance in this respect, suggesting that the Old Birch Island people had not long been under the influence of the Roman Catholic Church. Since Old Birch Island lay on the Mackinac-Montreal trade route, it could be expected that trade goods would come to the region

[28] Quimby, 1936, p. 21. [29] Kidd, 1949. [30] *Ibid.*, p. 3.

soon after their appearance in the eastern centers, and an early date is therefore preferable for Grave 18 and its contents, that is to say, sometime before 1800, and probably as early as 1780. This would mean that the use of the north end of Old Birch Island as a cemetery was known in the area at that time, even though some of the graves may have been made half a century or more previously. It is hardly deniable that this cemetery was known to the Indians occupying the village on Great Cloche Island, visited by Henry in 1761.[31] This village was only 4 miles distant from Old Birch Island (Map 4). These facts must be taken into consideration with the probability that the residents of Birch Island Reserve, on Cloche Peninsula, are descendants of the inhabitants of the village described by Henry. His unfortunate experience at that village, in which he was forced to give up some of the alcoholic liquors he was carrying to Mackinac for trade,[32] was related in 1939 by John Walker of Birch Island Reserve, with considerable agreement but some variations from Henry's account, as a story which had been preserved in his family. There was no indication that Henry's book was known to Walker or to any other residents of Birch Island Reserve.

In any event the Indians of this Reserve formerly lived, by their own account, on the south end of Old Birch Island, and that is the origin of the name of their present Reserve, which is not on an island but on the central and northern part of Cloche Peninsula. Statements as to the period of their occupation of Old Birch Island are vague, but it would seem to have been 75 or 100 years ago. Eventually, they moved to the mainland (Pl. I, Fig. 1) directly opposite the west side of Old Birch Island, and this land is today a part of the Reserve, with a few farms and maple sugar camps. The village of the Reserve is at the narrowest part of Cloche Peninsula between the westward extending arm of McGregor Bay and North Channel, at the railroad station known as Poncet. The east shore of Old Birch Island faces McGregor Bay proper, which is defined on the south by McGregor Point, the north line of Baie Fine (Map 2).

[31] Henry, 1809, p. 33. [32] *Ibid.*, pp. 33–34.

The word "Poncet" is a reference to Father Joseph Antoine Poncet, who spent the winter of 1648–49 on Manitoulin Island, going there from the mission of Ste Marie I.[33] There is no record of the exact place where Father Poncet carried on his missionary work, but it was among Algonquian Indians along the north shore of Lake Huron and on Manitoulin Island.[34] There is today a strong tradition on the island that its Indian inhabitants were first introduced to Christianity at the head of Thomas Bay on the southeast shore about 4 miles east of the entrance to South Bay. A few sparse signs of occupation were found there in 1940. Poncet station on the railroad appears to be a designation given in commemoration of the work of this Jesuit, not because of any record of his presence at that place. While there can be no doubt that the present inhabitants of Birch Island Reserve are descendants of a group that formerly lived on Old Birch Island, search for evidences of tillage and other activities at the south end revealed nothing. It is more likely that this occupation was at the north end where there is better soil. But the ultimate removal to the mainland opposite the west side of the Island was to the nearest arable land. The land north of the island is quartzite with no soil of any kind. There is a reference to "less than one hundred" Indians living on Birch Island in 1895,[35] but inquiry has not brought forth any further details.

The residents of Birch Island Reserve call themselves Ojibway, and the native language is the Ottawa-Ojibway variant of Central Algonquian. This group appears to have had a long residence in the northern Georgian Bay region, in contrast to the Indians of Wekwemikong Reserve on the east end of Manitoulin Island, who are mainly Ottawa, descendants of Indians who came to that island from Michigan, largely from the Cross Village area, after the War of 1812. The residents interviewed at Wekwemikong said that their ancestors were brought to Manitoulin Island by a Father Proulx, but gave no further details. Manitoulin Island had, however, been the home of the Ottawa Indians since before 1640,[36] and one of the first names

[33] Jones, 1909, pp. 390–91. [34] *Ibid.*, p. 390.

[35] Burdon, 1895, p. 18.

[36] *Jesuit Relations*, 18: 229, 231; 55: 141–43.

given to it by Europeans was "Isle des Ontaous."[37] The Birch Island Indians may well be descendants of one of the Ojibway groups recorded for the north shore of Georgian Bay in early historic times. Such were the Amikwa in 1640,[38] the Saulteur in 1746,[39] the Mississauga in 1748,[40] and the Nipissing or Nipissiriniens in 1670 and 1671.[41] The reference to the Mississauga describes them as living in a village on "Cloche" or "La Cloche" Island, which was known as Chibaouinani, translated by Jones as "passage-way." This same word is the former Ojibway name for the village of Killarney, 20 miles east of Great Cloche Island, and "Cheboygan" is evidently a derivative. While all three of these localities are characterized by narrow channels, it is to be noted that Chibaouinani is very close to Tchibaiinini, which in a liberal translation on the basis of Baraga's rendering[42] would be "burial ground." In this connection it should be stated that despite the early references to villages on Great Cloche Island an exhaustive search, continued intermittently over several seasons, failed to disclose anything more in the way of refuse material than a few animal bones on the sides of the low bluff bordering the swale between Great Cloche and Little Cloche islands (Pl. IV, Fig. 2). This is about a quarter of a mile south of the cemetery on Great Cloche Island.[43]

The period during which Old Birch Island Cemetery was used suggests that the ancestors of some of the present inhabitants of the region were the users, but the only artifact found on the site which can be linked with a historically known group points to a different group. The effigy tobacco pipe from Grave No. 3 recalls Iroquoian forms.[44] Pipes of this type were found at the site of the Huron Mission of Ste Marie I,[45] but this specimen

[37] Perrot, 1911, p. 221. [38] *Jesuit Relations*, 18: 231.

[39] Anonymous, 1858, p. 119.

[40] Mooney, 1907, p. 909; Jones, 1907, p. 258; La Galissonière, 1858.

[41] *Jesuit Relations*, 55: 149.

[42] Baraga, 1878. [43] Greenman and Stanley, 1940, pp. 194–99.

[44] Parker, 1920, Pl. 48; West, 1934, Pls. 95, 128; Greenman, 1935, Fig. 22 A, Fig. 25, Nos. 3, 20, 21.

[45] Kidd, 1949, Pl. 148 and Fig. 27K.

from Old Birch Island is not sufficient by itself for cultural identification. There are many indications that Indians from lower Ontario and New York were often in the Georgian Bay region. In 1649–50 the Huron fled to Manitoulin Island before the onslaught of the other Iroquois,[46] and the island at that time bore the Iroquois name Ekaentoton, which has been translated as "island of castaways." [47] But the Manitoulin area was generally hostile country for Iroquois aside from the Huron, and it is unlikely that a group would stay long enough in one place to accumulate as many graves as there were at Old Birch Island.

This cemetery may more plausibly be referred to the Woodland Pattern in the Midwestern Taxonomic System,[48] because of the character of the native artifacts and the absence of all of the prominent and highly distinctive traits of late Iroquois as it is known in New York[49] and southern Ontario.[50] Iroquois cemeteries are characteristically on or adjoining their village sites,[51] and the sites are usually or almost always on arable land with many evidences of agricultural and domestic activities. While there is good soil a short distance south of the cemetery on Old Birch Island, there is no evidence that the island was ever occupied until the present century, and the main shore north of the island is the solid quartzite of the Laurentian highlands. Since stone and bone were still in use by the originators of this cemetery, if they were Iroquois it is strange that these materials were not present in the form of the characteristic unnotched triangular flint points, small awls of the leg bones of birds and small mammals, bone combs, gouges and flaking tools of antler, and bone beaming tools.[52]

The specific division of the Woodland Pattern most strongly suggested by the Old Birch Island data is the Point Peninsula

[46] *Jesuit Relations*, 36: 189. [47] Jones, 1909, pp. 198–200.

[48] McKern, 1939, pp. 301–13; Anonymous, 1943, pp. 400–593.

[49] Parker, 1920, pp. 207–37, 246–302. [50] Wintemberg, 1939.

[51] *Ibid.*, p. 57; Parker, 1920, p. 248 and Pl. 70.

[52] Parker, 1920, Pls. 76, 88, 98, 99, 118, Fig. 26; Wintemberg, 1939, Pl. III, Nos. 3–8; Pl. X, Nos. 6–10.

Focus of the Vine Valley Aspect. The Point Peninsula is known from a large number of sites in New York and Ontario, around the shores of Lake Ontario and on inland lakes and rivers,[53] and although the record of this culture is mainly a mortuary one an adaptation to a lacustrine environment is abundantly indicated. The Old Birch Island traits which are prominent in the Point Peninsula are the side-notched projectile point with its coating of red ochre,[54] tubular marine shell beads,[55] oval pebble whetstones,[56] bone harpoons with unilateral barbs and line hole near the proximal barb,[57] long slender bone awl with head carved,[58] spindle-shaped slate object (flat instead of round in cross section in the Point Peninsula),[59] the use of boulders in graves,[60] fire-making sets as mortuary offerings,[61] placing of grave goods on the side walls of graves,[62] and damaging of grave goods in cremation fires.[63] Bundle burial, flexion and cremation, as well as multiple burial, are also common to Old Birch Island Cemetery and sites of the Point Peninsula Focus.[64] The incised sandstone disk from Grave 1 (Pl. XXI, C, D) is closely paralleled only at the Bainbridge site of the Owasco Aspect in New York.[65] The Owasco Aspect is of the Woodland Pattern, but has many early, or at any rate crudely executed, Iroquoian features and is presented as a connecting link between the Iroquois proper and the Point Peninsula.[66]

The type of harpoon which is distinctive for the Point Peninsula is a multiple, unilaterally barbed type with "square" barbs,[67] but the tapering-barb type like that of Old Birch Is.

[53] Ritchie, 1944, Pl. 53.

[54] *Ibid.*, p. 175; Pl. 54, No. 28; Pl. 71, Nos. 5, 6, 11–12, 16, 25; Pl. 75, Nos. 4–7; Pl. 76, Nos. 24, 38, 39; Pl. 84, Nos. 1–7.

[55] *Ibid.*, Pl. 54, No. 4.

[56] *Ibid.*, Pl. 69, No. 33; Pl. 56, Nos. 8, 9; Pl. 85, No. 20.

[57] *Ibid.*, Pl. 61, No. 15. [58] *Ibid.*, Pl. 61, No. 11.

[59] *Ibid.*, Pl. 59, No. 28. [60] *Ibid.*, pp. 128, 178, 363.

[61] *Ibid.*, p. 364, Pl. 54, Nos. 5–7, 23, 29; Pl. 71, Nos. 33, 34, and p. 154.

[62] *Ibid.*, p. 160. [63] *Ibid.*, pp. 152–54.

[64] *Ibid.*, pp. 123, 125–26, 128, 134, 140, 152, 154, 166, 168, 170.

[65] *Ibid.*, Pl. 46, No. 7.

[66] *Ibid.*, Pl. 4; Ritchie and MacNeish, 1949, pp. 121–22.

[67] *Ibid.*, Pl. 61, No. 16.

land is present.[68] The multiple-bilaterally-barbed type of harpoon with tapering barb is[69] the most common Iroquois type, and the placing of the line hole well above the base of the harpoon, characterizing 2 of the specimens from Old Birch Island and 4 from Kipp Island and the Point Peninsula site,[70] is indicated for the Iroquois only at the Sidney-Mackay site in Simcoe County, Ontario, which is probably an early historic Tionontati site, before 1620.[71]

These similarities between Old Birch Island and the Point Peninsula are far from conclusive, but they outweigh any claim for diagnostic rating that can be made for the effigy pipe from Grave 3. This pipe, with its constricted and perforated base, is not a good Iroquois type. It recalls the Micmac type said to have been in use by the Micmac Indians of Nova Scotia at the time of their first contact with Europeans.[72] Further, the value of one lone diagnostic Iroquois trait at Old Birch Island would be held in serious question because the site lies on a widely used trade route.

The Point Peninsula Focus is one division of the Vine Valley Aspect of the Woodland Pattern.[73] Its chronological position in the New York cultures is intermediate between an archaic period and a late prehistoric period.[74] Old Birch Island belongs to the historic period and Grave 18, at least, to a rather late date. If Old Birch Island is taken to represent an evolved Point Peninsula culture, the matter of the amount of time since the existence of the latter in its classic form assumes importance. Point Peninsula is regarded as contemporary with late Hopewellian, with the Uren site in Canada, and with the Heinisch Mound of the so-called Intrusive Culture,[75] with which it is closely related.[76] Ritchie[77] carried the Point Peninsula as far as the middle of the late prehistoric period in New York, which he

[68] *Ibid.*, Pl. 61, No. 15.

[69] Wintemberg, 1936, Pl. I, Figs. 22, 24, 26, and pp. 28–29.

[70] Ritchie, 1944, Pl. 61, Nos. 15, 17; Pl. 76, Nos. 2, 17.

[71] Wintemberg, 1946, Pl. XIX, A, No. 18, and p. 181.

[72] West, 1934, p. 228, and Pl. 172, Figs. 1, 4; Parker, 1922, Fig. 5.

[73] Ritchie, 1944, p. 114. [74] *Ibid.*, Pl. 2. [75] Griffin, 1946, Fig. 1.

[76] Ritchie, 1944, p. 117. [77] *Ibid.*, Pl. 4.

dated at A.D. 1400, with its beginning a little after A.D. 1000 in the intermediate period. At Killarney, Ontario, about 20 miles east of Old Birch Island, there is under excavation at the present time a site which is datable, by reference to the post-glacial tilting of the Great Lakes basin, at about A.D. 500.[78] The pottery in the topsoil component of this site was first placed in the Brewerton Focus of the Laurentian Aspect[79] on the basis of its occurrence in the upper levels of the Robinson and Oberlander sites in New York.[80] Subsequently, that ceramic type came to be regarded as belonging to the Vine Valley Aspect, and to the Point Peninsula Focus of that aspect, rather than to the Laurentian.[81] In other traits beside this pottery, the Killarney Bay topsoil component shows none of the diagnostic features of the Point Peninsula, but it lies on top of another component the materials of which are for the most part in water-laid gravels, and are markedly Adena-like.[82] Furthermore, during recent excavation the proximal end of a tubular pipe made of pipestone of the type found at Beech Bottom, West Virginia, in an Adena mound,[83] was recovered from the topsoil near a burial which had a necklace of copper beads of the rolled type characteristic of the Point Peninsula.[84] It may be that the topsoil component of Killarney Bay 1 represents the Vine Valley Aspect at a time before the 2 foci, Middlesex and Point Peninsula, had become differentiated. But while this component was almost certainly contemporaneous with the later stages of the formation of the beach on which it lies, it could have lasted long after that, as is suggested by the late date allowed for the Point Peninsula in New York.[85]

Certainly in the Killarney area, cultures can be shown to have continued in existence for thousands of years, and there is a definite flavor of evolutionary development there as in the Woodland cultures of New York. The topsoil component of Killarney Bay 1 is present in a nonceramic context at Chikani-

[78] Greenman and Stanley, 1941, p. 312. [79] Greenman, 1946, p. 316.
[80] Ritchie, 1940, pp. 47–48, 85–86. [81] *Ibid.*, 1944, p. 164.
[82] Greenman, 1946, p. 316; 1932, Fig. 2; Haag, 1940, pp. 75–79.
[83] Bache and Satterthwaite, 1930, Pl. IX, No. 2.
[84] Ritchie, 1944, pp. 125, 128. [85] *Ibid.*, Pl. 4.

sing Creek 1, 4 miles away on a raised beach with an apparent antiquity of some 2600 years.[86] There is evidence also of a third component at Killarney Bay 1 on a part of the site not yet excavated, consisting of the recent find on the surface of a ground slate point familiar in the Laurentian Aspect of the archaic pattern[87] in New York. These considerations indicate that activities in the Killarney area many centuries before the use of Old Birch Island Cemetery were quite capable of being carried on to that late date and of producing there a cultural assemblage some of the elements of which in New York go to make up the Point Peninsula Focus.

The trait list of Old Birch Island offers but a tenuous identification at best, but no more so than might be expected of a rather ancient pre-Columbian culture in a survival into historic times. Some of the traits of this cemetery can be regarded as translations into the terms of the historic and European technology of pre-Columbian native types. This is certainly true of the fire-making sets, familiar in the pre-Columbian context as lumps of iron pyrites associated with pieces of flint. At Old Birch Island the pyrites are replaced by the manufactured iron strike-a-lights in 3 graves. Other traits may be interpreted in the same way. The 4 iron rods with wooden handles would be familiar enough in a modern workshop, but those from this site might be descended from the copper rods with bone handles which characterize the Hopewellian[88] and are found in the Point Peninsula Focus.[89] Again, the boxlike wooden cribs forming the sides of some of the Old Birch Island graves may be the historic version, directly resulting from the acquisition of superior wood-cutting tools like the iron axes, of the stone slab-cyst graves of the Point Peninsula.[90] Boulders and slabs are constructional features of many of the graves of that focus in New York; in one instance they protruded through the sod on

[86] Greenman and Stanley, 1941, p. 313.

[87] Ritchie, 1944, p. 246; Pl. 148, No. 20.

[88] Shetrone and Greenman, 1931, Fig. 34.

[89] Ritchie, 1944, Pl. 56, Nos. 38, 39; Pl. 61, No. 5; Pl. 62, No. 6.

[90] *Ibid.*, pp. 128, 140, 152, 154, 158, 166, 168, 170.

the surface.[91] There is no possibility, however, that the stones around the graves at Old Birch Island were originally beneath the surface, for the surface of that site, buried beneath a thick mantle of leaf mold, was never seen after abandonment of the cemetery until the year of its excavation. Finally, the large number of glass beads at Old Birch Island is answered in the Point Peninsula by an abundance of copper beads.[92] But the frequent placing of brass pails in the graves of Old Birch Island is not a Point Peninsula trait expressed with the native pots, since pottery was not, except in one questionable case, placed in the graves of that culture.[93]

The Point Peninsula people were the inhabitants of a very definite ecological zone, the shores of large bodies of water, and Old Birch Island is an extreme case in this respect. The preference of the Point Peninsula people for islands and the shores of lakes, swamps, and large rivers is seen in such sites in New York as Kipp Island on a marsh of Seneca River, "Burial Ridge" on Staten Island, the Sea Breeze site and the Point Peninsula site on Lake Ontario, the Lake Muskalonge site, the Bay of Quinte site on Lake Ontario in Canada, the Vinette site on Oneida River,[94] and, in Michigan, the West Twin Lake site in Montmorency County.[95]

Old Birch Island Cemetery cannot with finality be placed in any cultural division below the pattern level. It yielded 2 artifacts which come very close to being diagnostic traits for 2 fundamentally different patterns in the taxonomic system, namely the tobacco pipe and the ochre-stained projectile point. The latter is highly specific for the Point Peninsula in view of the presence of the type in that culture and the great abundance of triangular, thin, unnotched blades in caches imbedded in red ochre,[96] from which the notched points were rather obviously made. But this point from Old Birch Island lay at the edge of an unoccupied grave, unassociated with any of the other

[91] *Ibid.*, p. 173. [92] *Ibid.*, pp. 125, 128. [93] *Ibid.*, p. 175.

[94] *Ibid.*, pp. 132, 119, 128, 166, 175, 178, 160, respectively.

[95] Hinsdale, 1928, 1929.

[96] Ritchie, 1944, pp. 117, 150; Pl. 70, Nos. 1–29.

artifacts on the site, and the general type, though not coated with red ochre, does occur in the Iroquois Aspect.[97] Nevertheless, its diagnostic value would seem to be higher than that of the pipe.

Whether or not Old Birch Island Cemetery represents a survival into historic times of the culture of Point Peninsula, the evidence is definitely on the side of the Woodland Pattern. It is most likely that the users of this cemetery belonged to one of the Algonquian-speaking groups whose home had for generations been along the bays and islands of the north shore of Georgian Bay, and their descendants may still reside in that region.

REFERENCES

Anonymous

1855 State of the British Plantations in America, in 1721. *In* Documents Relative to the Colonial History of the State of New York. Albany: Weed, Parsons and Co. V: 591–630.

1858 Journal of Occurrences in Canada, 1746, 1747. *Ibid.*, X: 89–132.

1922 Indian Graves Unearthed at Charlestown. *In* Rhode Island Hist. Soc. Coll., XV, No. 1: 18–19, pl. opp. p. 24.

1943 The First Archaeological Conference on the Woodland Pattern. Amer. Antiq., VIII, No. 4: 393–400.

Bache, Charles, and Linton Satterthwaite

1930 The Excavation of an Indian Mound at Beach Bottom, West Virginia. Journ. Mus. Univ. Pa., XXI, Nos. 3–4: 133–88.

Baraga, Frederick

1878 A Dictionary of the Otchipwe Language, Explained in English. Montreal: Beauchemin and Valois.

Beck, Horace C.

1928 Classification and Nomenclature of Beads and Pendants. Archaeologia, 77: 1–76.

Bloomfield, Leonard

1933 Language. New York: Henry Holt and Co.

Burdon, Harold Nelson

1895 Manitoulin; or, Five Years of Church Work among Ojibway Indians and Lumbermen, Resident upon That Island or in Its Vicinity. London: Simkin, Marshall, Hamilton, Kent & Co., Ltd.

[97] Wintemberg, 1939, Pl. III, Nos. 9–11; 1936, Pl. I, No. 3.

Cadillac, Antoine de la Mothe
1895 Cadillac Papers. *In* Mich. Pioneer and Hist. Coll., 33.

Clare, and Others
1857 Representation of the Lords of Trade on the State of Indian Affairs. Letter signed by Clare, Soame Jenyns, Thomas Robinson, Wm. Fitzherbert, Ed: Eliot, dated March 7, 1768. *In* Documents Relative to the Colonial History of the State of New York. Albany: Wead, Parsons and Co. VIII: 19–31.

Colden, Cadwallader
1856 Lieutenant-Governor Colden to the Lords of Trade. Letter Dated Oct. 12, 1764. *In* Documents Relative to the Colonial History of the State of New York. Albany: Wead, Parsons and Co., VII: 667–70.

Greenman, Emerson F.
1935 Excavation of the Reeve Village Site, Lake County, Ohio. Ohio State Archaeol. and Hist. Quart., XLIV, No. 1: 5–64.
1946 The Killarney Sequence and Its Old World Connections. Papers Mich. Acad., XXXII: 313–19.

Greenman, Emerson F., and George M. Stanley
1940 A Geologically Dated Camp Site, Georgian Bay, Ontario. Amer. Antiq., V: 194–99.
1941 Two Post-Nipissing Sites, near Killarney, Ontario. *Ibid.*, VI, No. 4: 305–13.

Griffin, James B.
1946 Cultural Change and Continuity in Eastern United States Archaeology. *In* Man in Northeastern North America, ed. Frederick Johnson. Papers Robt. S. Peabody Found. Archaeol., 3: 37–95.

Haag, William G.
1940 A Description of the Wright Site Pottery. *In* The Wright Mounds, by Wm. S. Webb, Dept. Anthropol. and Archaeol., Univ. Ky., Repts. in Anthropol., 5: 75–79.

Henry, Alexander
1809 Travels and Adventures in Canada and The Indian Territories between the Years 1760 and 1776. New York: I. Riley.

Hinsdale, Wilbert B.
1928 Indian Mounds, West Twin Lake, Montmorency County, Michigan. Papers Mich. Acad., X: 91–101.
1929 Report of Archaeological Field Work in the Summer of 1928 in Montmorency, Newaygo and Lake Counties, Michigan. *Ibid.*, XII: 127–35.

Jesuit Relations
1896–1901 The Jesuit Relations and Allied Documents, ed. Reuben G. Thwaites. Cleveland: Burrows Bros.

Jones, Arthur Edward

1909 "ȣ Endake Ehen" or Old Huronia. Fifth Rept. Bur. Archives Province of Ontario. Toronto.

Jones, William

1907, 1910 Chibaouinani. *In* Handbook of the American Indians North of Mexico, ed. Frederick W. Hodge. Bur. Amer. Ethnol. Bull., Pt. 1, 30: 258.

Kidd, Kenneth E.

1949 The Excavation of Ste. Marie I. Toronto: Univ. Toronto Press.

La Galissonière

1858 Letter from M. de la Gallissonière to Count de Maurepas, Dated October 23, 1748. *In* Documents Relating to the Colonial History of the State of New York. Albany: Wead, Parsons and Co. X: 181–85.

McKern, W. C.

1939 The Midwestern Taxonomic Method as an Aid to Archaeological Culture Study. Amer. Antiq., IV, No 4: 301–14.

Mooney, James, and Cyrus Thomas

1907, 1910 Mississauga. *In* Handbook of the American Indians North of Mexico, ed. Frederick W. Hodge. Bur. Amer. Ethnol. Bull., Pt 1, 30: 909–10.

Old Admiralty Chart, No. 1213

Hydrographic and Map Service, Surv. and Eng. Branch, Dept. Mines and Resources, Ottawa.

Parker, Arthur C.

1920 The Archeological History of New York. N. Y. State Mus. Bull., Nos. 235 and 236. Pts. 1 and 2.

Perrot, Nicolas

1911 Memoir on the Manners, Customs, and Religion of the Savages of North America (English trans.) *In* The Indian Tribes of the Upper Mississippi Valley and Region of the Great Lakes, by Emma Helen Blair. I: 29, 31–272.

Quimby, George I., Jr.

1936 Notes on Indian Trade Silver Ornaments in Michigan. Papers Mich. Acad., XXII: 15–24.

Ritchie, William A.

1940 Two Prehistoric Village Sites at Brewerton, New York. Res. Records Rochester Mus. Arts and Sci., No. 5.

1944 The Pre-Iroquoian Occupations of New York. Rochester Mus. Mem., I.

Ritchie, William A., and Richard S. MacNeish

1949 The Pre-Iroquoian Pottery of New York State. Amer. Antiq., XV, No. 2: 97–124.

SHETRONE, HARRY C., and EMERSON F. GREENMAN
1931 Explorations of the Seip Group of Prehistoric Earthworks. Ohio Archaeol. and Hist. Quart., XL, No. 3: 343–509.
WEST, GEORGE A.
1934 Tobacco, Pipes and Smoking Customs of the American Indians. Bull. Public Mus. Milwaukee, Pts. I and II, Vol. 17.
WINTEMBERG, W. J.
1936 Roebuck Prehistoric Village Site, Grenville County, Ontario. Nat. Mus. Can. Anthropol. Ser., No. 19, Bull., No. 83, pp. 1–178.
1939 Lawson Prehistoric Village Site, Middlesex County, Ontario. Can. Dept. Mines and Resources, Mines and Geol. Branch. *Ibid.*, No. 25, Bull., No. 94.
1946 The Sidney-Mackay Village Site. Amer. Antiq., XI, No. 3: 154–82.

PLATES

PLATE I

Fig. 1. West shore of Old Birch Island, with mainland of Cloche Peninsula in the right distance.

Fig. 2. Strait between Great Cloche Island and Little Cloche Island, from Dreamer's Rock.

PLATE II

Fig. 1. Swift Current and Cloche Channel.

Fig. 2. Rock bearing cup marks on Great Cloche Island.

PLATE III

FIG. 1. French River, main entrance, about a mile inside, looking north.

FIG. 2. Entrance to Bad River Channel of French River, looking north.

PLATE IV

FIG. 1. Killarney Channel, looking west.

FIG. 2. South end of strait between Great and Little Cloche islands.

PLATE V

Fig. 1. Grondine Point.

Fig. 2. Collins Inlet.

PLATE VI

Aerial view of Voyageur Channel entrance.

PLATE VII

Fig. 1. Indian Bight, north of Grondine Point.

Fig. 2. Main entrance of French River, from Georgian Bay.

PLATE VIII

FIG. 1. McGregor Bay and McGregor Point as seen from Dreamer's Rock, looking east.

FIG. 2. East arm of Cloche Channel, looking north from the site of the cemetery (LC 1) on Great Cloche Island.

PLATE IX

FIG. 1. McGregor Bay from Dreamer's Rock. Old Birch Island is in the distance, just to the right of the peak in the foreground.

FIG. 2. Poncet Station, the village on Birch Island Reserve, and Bay of Islands, looking west.

PLATE X

Fig. 1. Site of early historic cemetery on Great Cloche Island (LC 1).

Fig. 2. The general area of the Indian village on Great Cloche Island visited by Alexander Henry, looking south from the early historic cemetery. The strait between Great Cloche and Little Cloche islands is in the distance.

PLATE XI

Fig. 1. Grave 19, before excavation.

Fig. 2. Grave 3, exposed.

PLATE XII

FIG. 1. Grave 2, exposed.

FIG. 2. Grave 3, partly exposed.

PLATE XIII

FIG. 1. Grave 6, exposed.

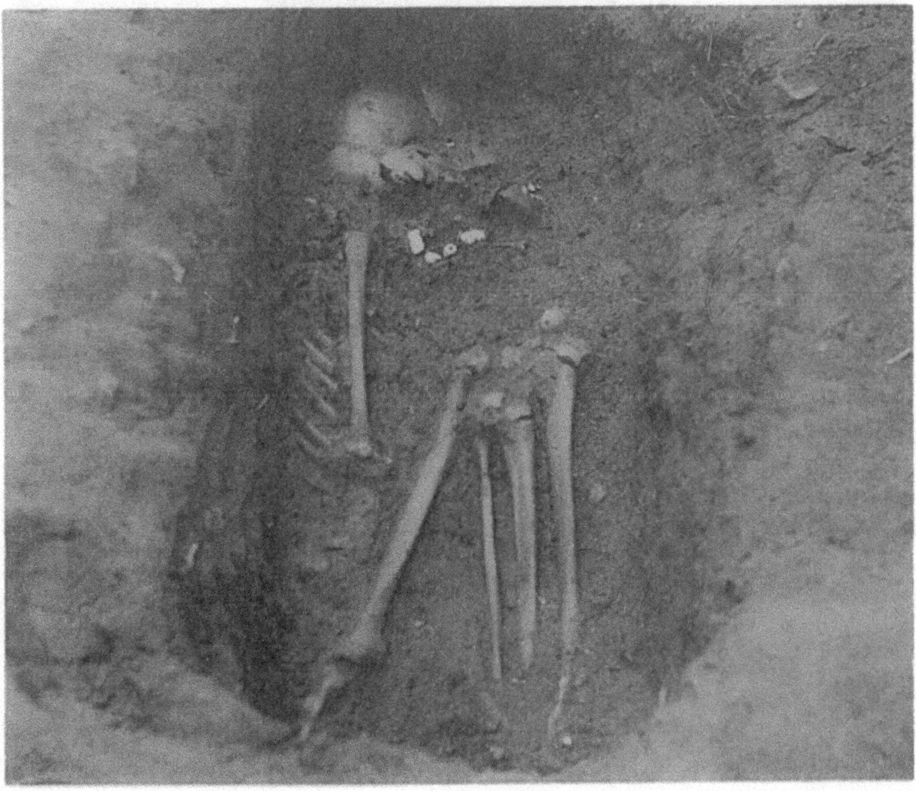

FIG. 2. Grave 8, exposed.

PLATE XIV

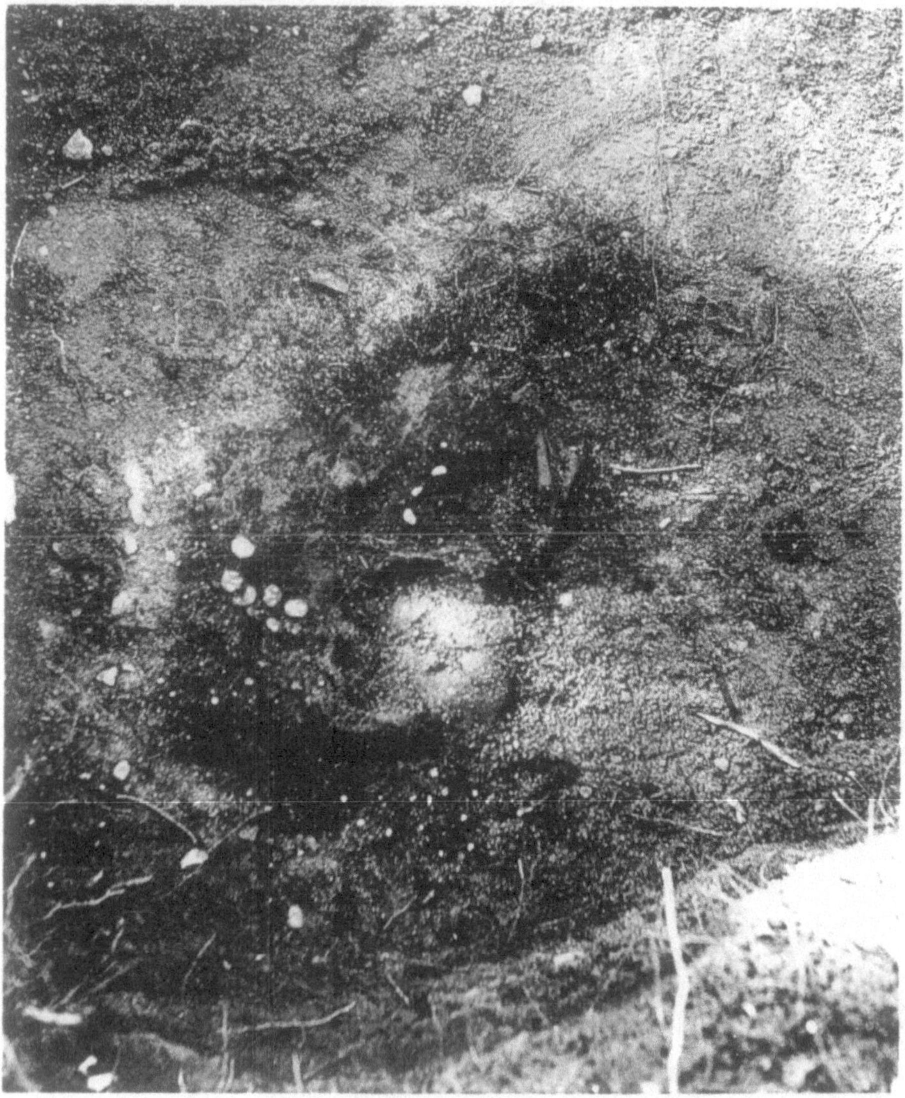

Grave 13, exposed.

PLATE XV

FIG. 1. Grave 19, exposed.

FIG. 2. Grave 15, exposed.

PLATE XVI

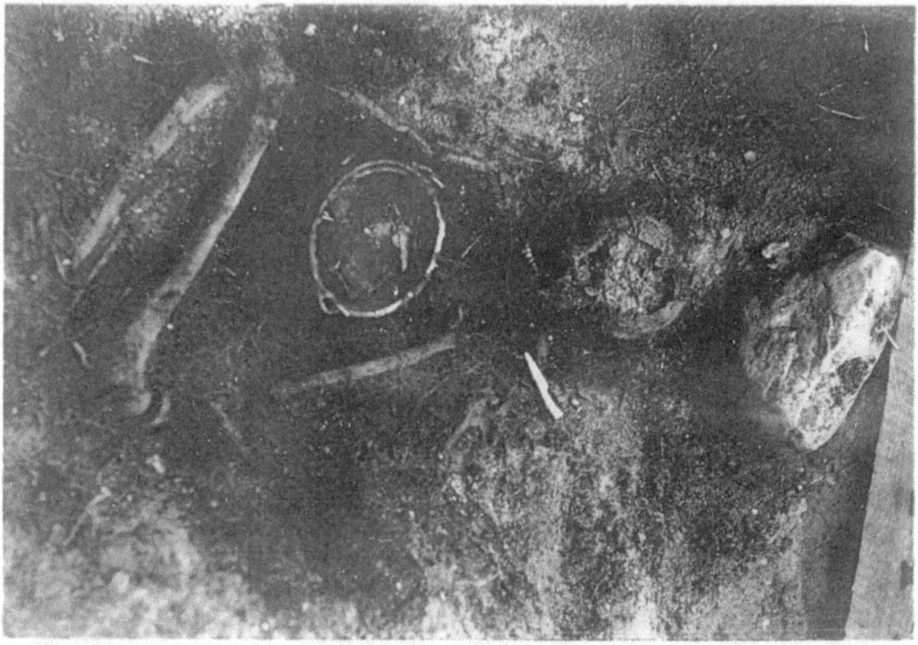

Fig. 1. Grave 1, exposed.

Fig. 2. Grave 18, exposed.

PLATE XVII

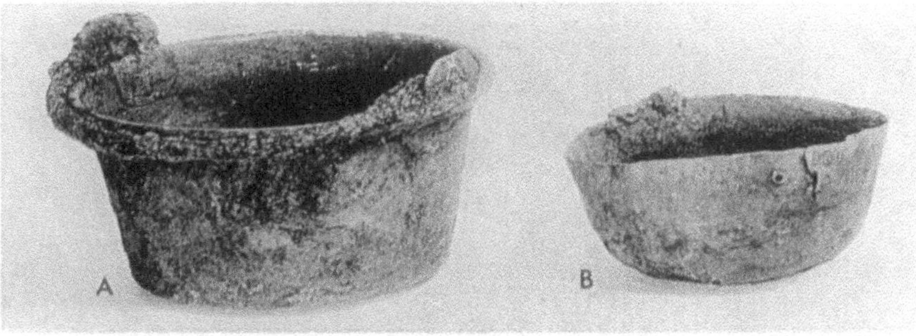

Fig. 1. *A*, brass pail (Grave 18, No. 21827); *B*, brass pail (Grave 19, No. 21831).

Fig. 2. *A*, brass pail (Grave 6, No. 21774); *B*, wooden cup (Grave 6, No. 21777).

Fig. 3. *A*, wooden ladle bowl (Grave 3, No. 21759); *B*, wooden tray (Grave 1, No. 21720).

PLATE XVIII

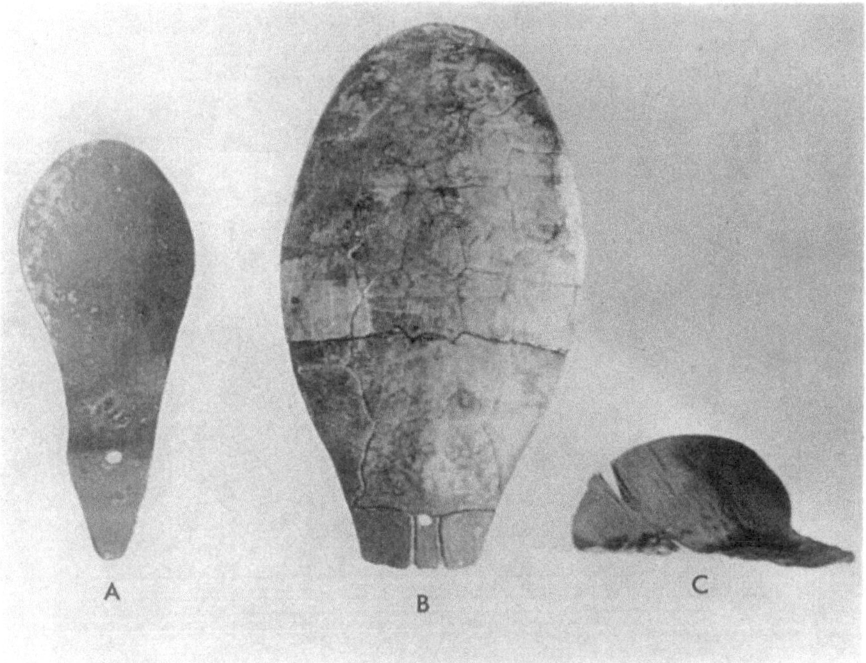

FIG. 1. *A*, brass spoon (Grave 3, No. 21746); *B*, ladle of turtle shell (Grave 3, No. 21760); *C*, wood (Grave 6, No. 21772).

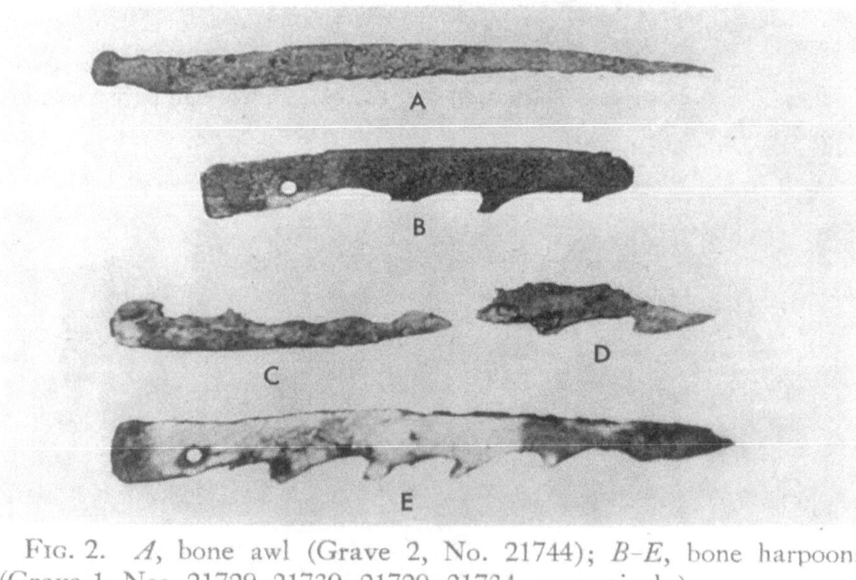

FIG. 2. *A*, bone awl (Grave 2, No. 21744); *B–E*, bone harpoons (Grave 1, Nos. 21729, 21730, 21729, 21734, respectively).

PLATE XIX

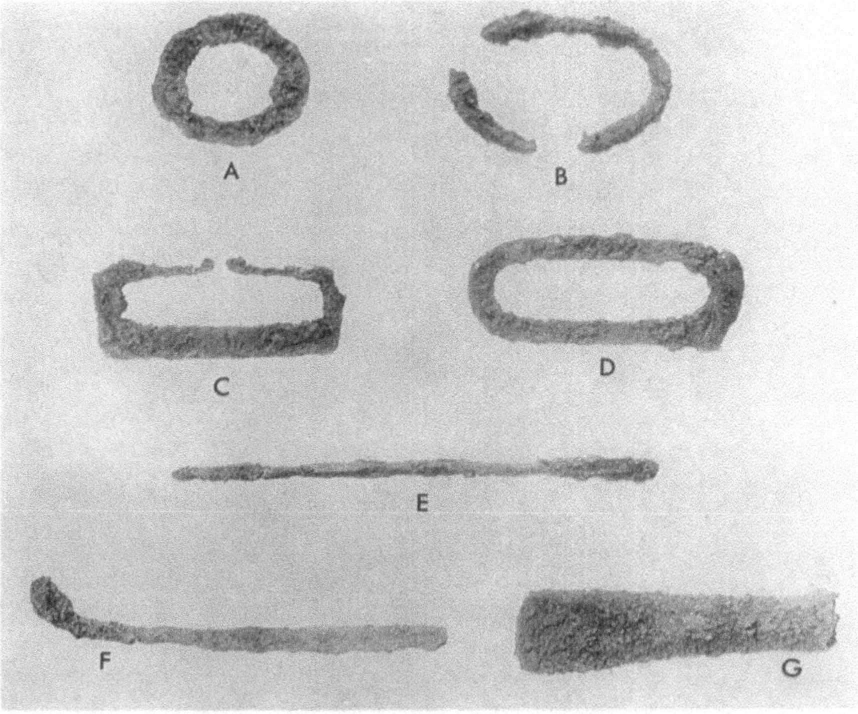

FIG. 1. *A*, iron strike-a-light (Grave 18, No. 21828); *B*, iron strike-a-light (Grave 1, No. 21736); *C*, iron strike-a-light (Grave 19, No. 21839); *D*, iron strike-a-light (Grave 17, No. 21818); *E*, iron awl (Grave 1, No. 21731); *F*, curved iron knife (Grave 1, No. 21738); *G*, iron chisel (Grave 1, No. 21737).

FIG. 2. *A*, iron knife (Grave 19, No. 21841); *B*, iron knife (Grave 17, No. 21822); *C*, iron knife (Grave 3, No. 21754).

PLATE XX

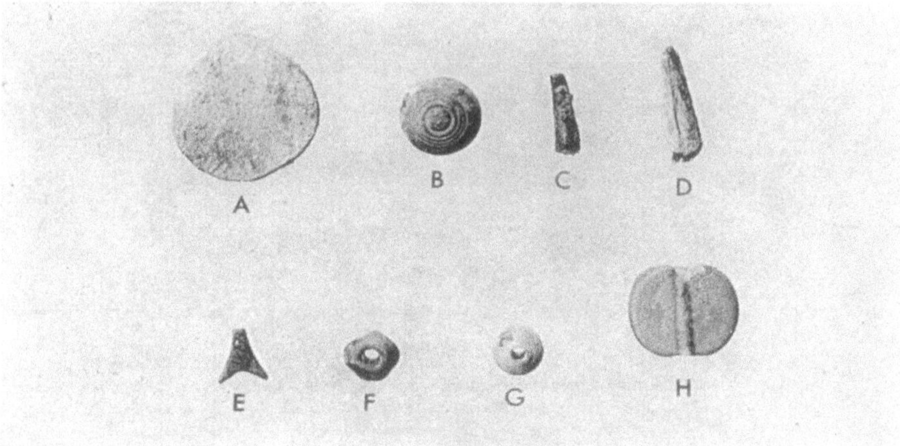

FIG. 1. *A*, lead disk (Grave 19, No. 21845); *B*, brass button (Grave 5, No. 21767); *C*, brass bangle (Grave 5, No. 21765); *D*, brass bangle (Grave 17, No. 21804); *E*, catlinite ornament (Grave 5, No. 21766); *F*, glass bead (Grave 8, No. 21870); *G*, glass bead (Grave 8, No. 21780); *H*, blue glass bead from Green Point Mound, Saginaw, Michigan, similar to those in Plate XXIV.

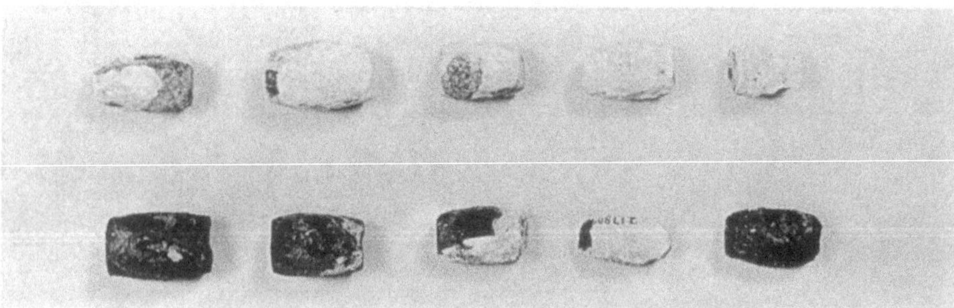

FIG. 2. Tubular marine shell beads (Grave 8, No. 21780).

PLATE XXI

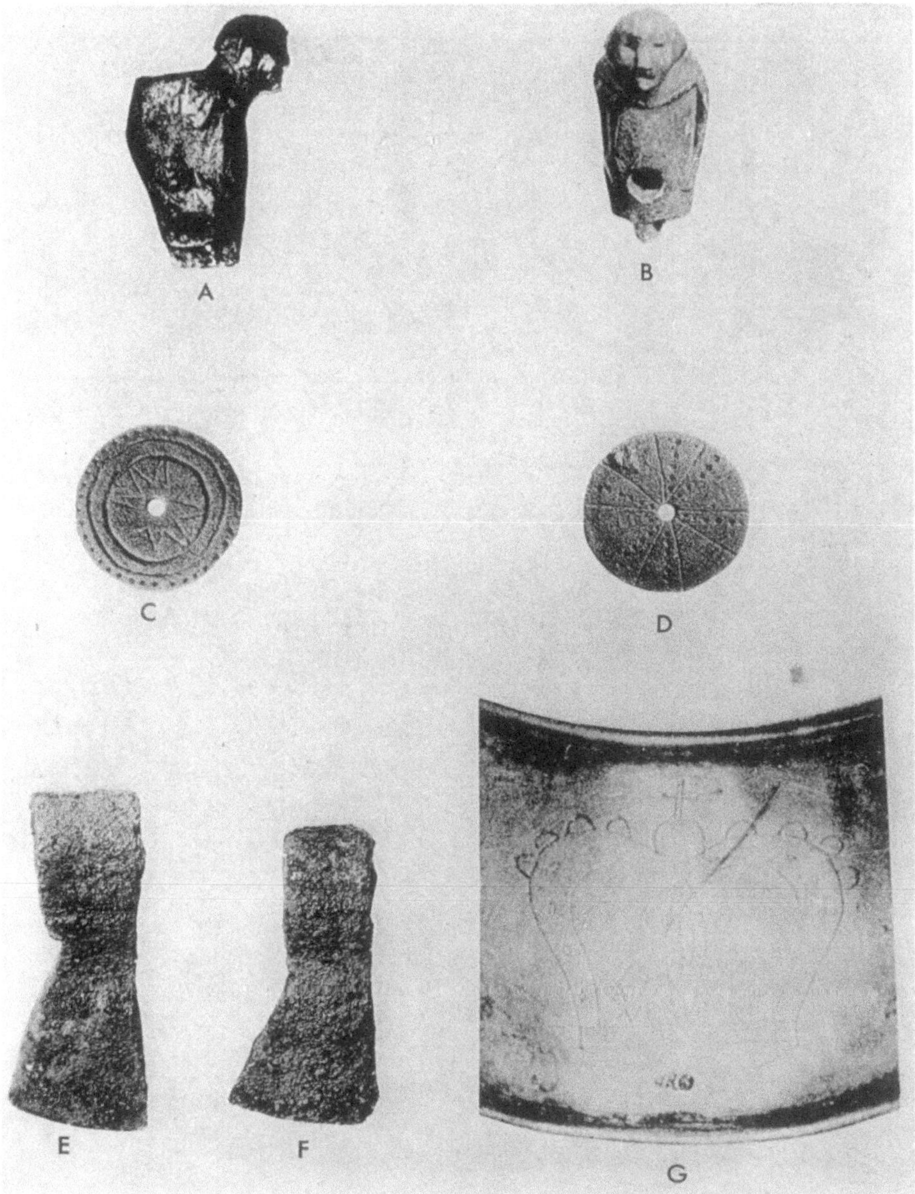

A–B, side and front views, respectively, of clay human-effigy tobacco pipe (Grave 3, No. 21750); *C–D*, both faces of an incised sandstone disk (Grave 1, No. 21726); *E*, iron axe (Grave 3, No. 21753); *F*, iron axe (Grave 17, No. 21806); *G*, enlarged section of silver crescent (Grave 18, No. 21826). See also text Figure 6. Scale not uniform.

PLATE XXII

FIG. 1. *A*, gorget of lead or pewter (Grave 6, No. 21773); *B*, crescent of silver (Grave 18, No. 21826); *C*, mirror, in wooden frame (Grave 17, Nos. 21808, 21809).

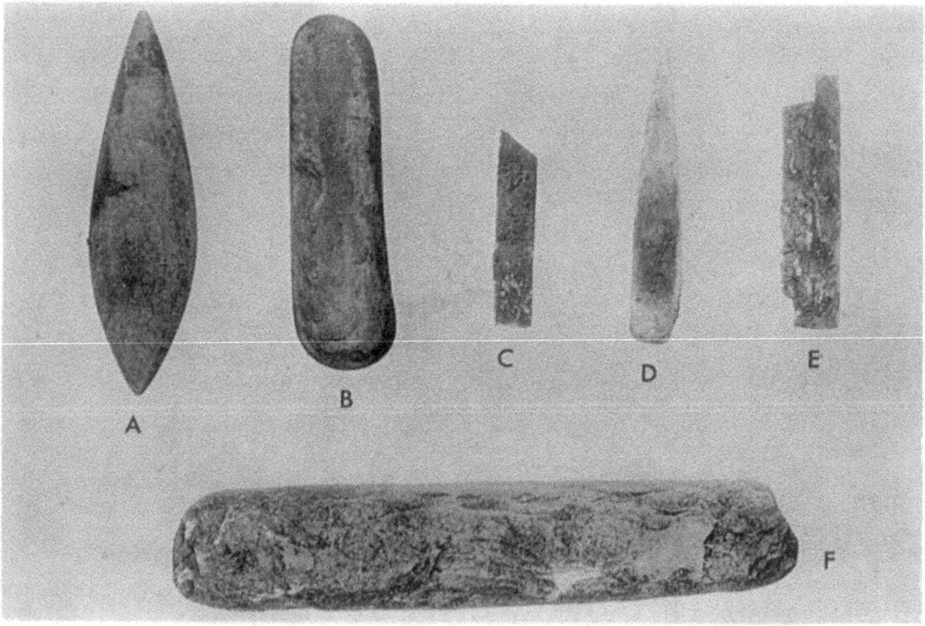

FIG. 2. *A*, slate spindle (Grave 1, No. 21725); *B*, pebble whetstone (Grave 3, No. 21749); *C*, strip of brass (Grave 1, No. 21723); *D*, punch, limestone (Grave 1, No. 21723); *E*, strip of brass (Grave 1, No. 21727); *F*, slate bar, surface (No. 21847).

PLATE XXIII

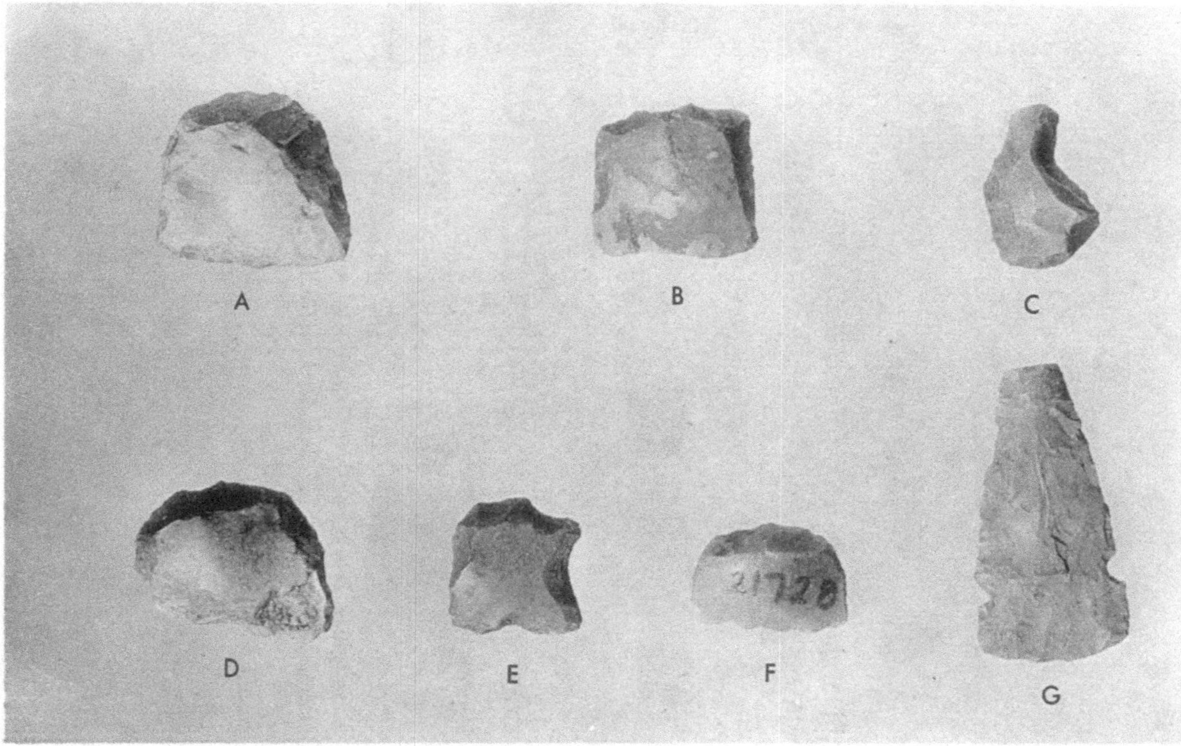

A, gunflint (Grave 3, No. 21751); *B*, gunflint (Grave 17, No. 21812); *C*, flint for strike-a-light (Grave 19, No. 21834); *D*, flint (Grave 3, No. 21747); *E*, strike-a-light flint (Grave 17, No. 21817); *F*, flint (Grave 1, No. 21728); *G*, projectile point coated with red ochre, near Grave 10, on surface (No. 21782).

PLATE XXIV

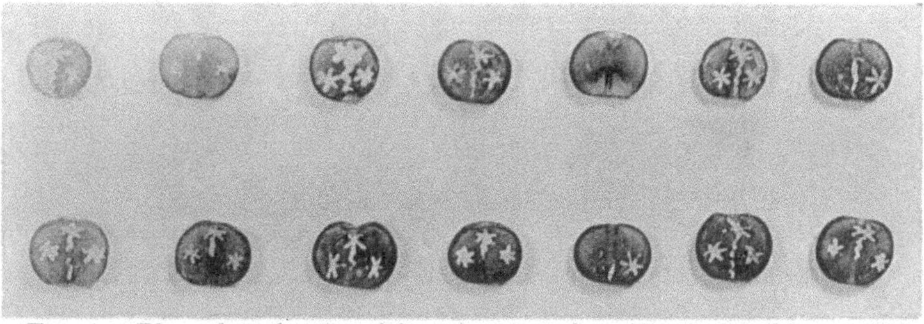

FIG. 1. Blue glass beads with painted design (Grave 13, Nos. 21785, 21787). Reverse side in Fig. 2. See also Pl. XXVI, *N*, *O*.

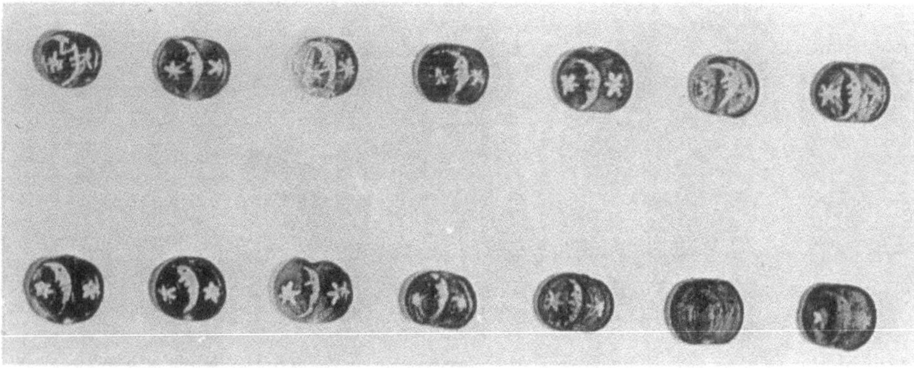

FIG. 2. Blue glass beads with painted design (Grave 13, Nos. 21785, 21787). Reverse side in Fig. 1. See also Pl. XXVI, *N*, *O*.

PLATE XXV

Fig. 1. *A* (No. 21770); *B* (No. 21832); *C* (No. 21802); *D* (No. 21703); *E* (No. 21703); *F* (No. 21775); *G* (No. 21771); *H* (No. 21705).

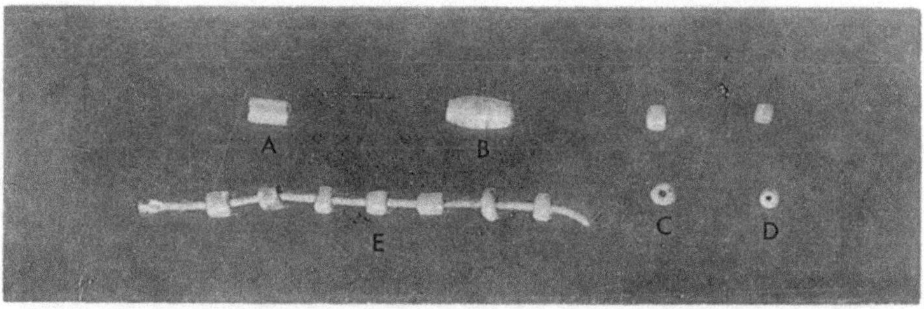

Fig. 2. *A* (No. 21852); *B* (No. 21704); *C* (No. 21802); *D* (No. 21775); *E* (No. 21701). C is medium, D is small, discoidal.

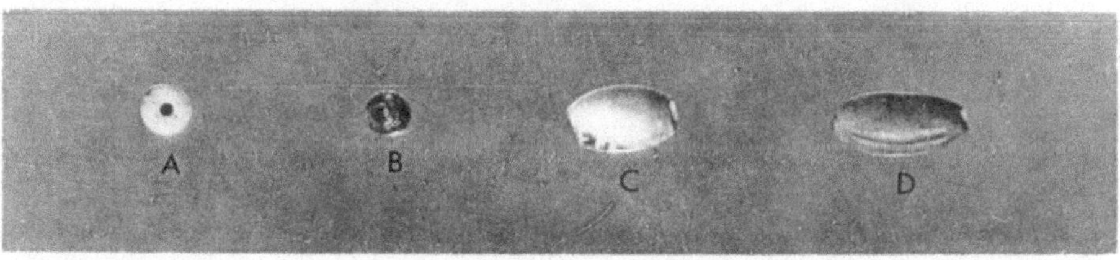

Fig. 3. *A* (No. 21732); *B* (No. 21704); *C* (No. 21789); *D* (No. 21792).

Types of glass beads.

PLATE XXVI

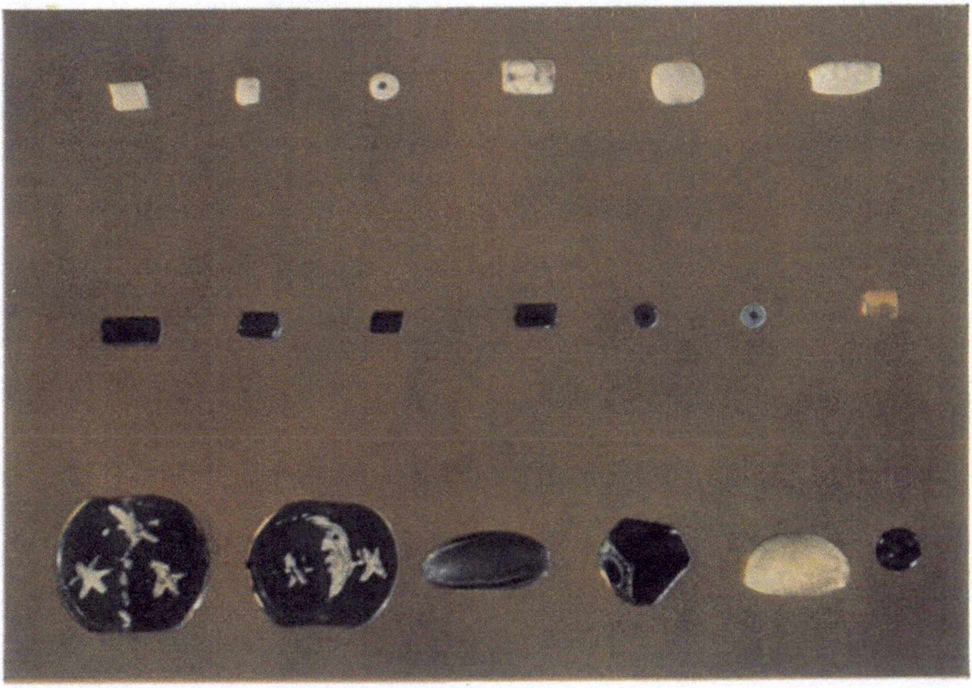

Colors of glass beads from Old Birch Island and Great Cloche Island.

Old Birch Island (from left to right and down): A (No. 21852); B (No. 21802); D (No. 21732); E (No. 21732); G (No. 21770); H (No. 21832); I (No. 21852); K (No. 21775); N (No. 21787); O (No. 21787); P (No. 21788); Q (No. 21780); R (No. 21789).

Great Cloche Island: C (No. 21701); F (No. 21704); J (No. 21705); L (No. 21705); M (No. 21705); S (No. 21704).